Henri-Dominique

Life of

SAINT MARY

MAGDALENE

Translated by
George G. Christian, OP

Reviewed by
Cajetan Cuddy, OP

Sainte Marie-Madeleine

par

Le R. P. H.-D.- LACORDAIRE
Des Frères Prêcheurs

Membre de l'Académie Française

PARIS

Librairie de Mme Ve Poussièlgue-Rusand
Rue Saint-Sulpice, 23

1860

Table of Contents 1

2

IN PRAISE OF PROVENCE

When the traveler goes down the slopes of the Rhône, at a certain moment, on the left, the mountains spread out, the horizon expands, the sky becomes clearer, the ground more luxuriant, the air fresher. This is Provence. Leaning against the Alps, it leaves them slowly by valleys, that little by little lose the harshness of the high peaks, and advances, like a headland of Greece and Italy, towards the sea that bathes all the famous shores. After the Rhône and the Alps, the Mediterranean forms the third belt, and its own river, the Durance, pours into its passes and plains with the impetuous speed of a flow that does not die away. One cannot look at this land without quickly recognizing a relationship of nature and history with the most celebrated regions of antiquity. Early on, Greek colonies brought to it the influence of the Orient; Rome, which gave it its name, left ruins worthy of that power which refused to no one a part of its grandeurs because it had enough of it for the universe. When the ancient world came to an end, for a long while Provence — rich in its memories, and richer still on its own — preserved its personality even in the breakup of things. It had its language, its poetry, its customs, its nationality, its glory — all those gifts that, in certain circumstances, make of a small country a large region. Then, when modern empires took their shape and delineated their territory, Provence — too weak to protect

4

itself against destiny — fell to France as a present from God. After having been for the ancients the west of beauty, it became for us the first port where our imagination meets Italy, Greece, Asia, all the places that enchant memory and all the names that move the heart.

But if nature and history have done much for Provence, perhaps religion has done even more for it. There are places made holy by a destiny lost in the secrets of eternity. Egypt saw the birth of Moses; Arabia still simmers from the lightning of Sinai; and the sands of its deserts have preserved a trace of the people of God; the Jordan opened up before that same people; from the cedars of Lebanon to the palm trees of Jericho, Palestine was to hear and see things that would be the everlasting talk of mankind. The Son of God was born on those shores; his Word taught the world there, and his blood flowed there, in order to save it. In its turn, Rome, the inheritor of everything, received within it walls the successor of Christ; its astonished Capitol gave way to the chaste ceremonies of victorious love, after long having served the bloody triumphs of war. There are the places consecrated by religion, the holy places, that, among others, we could believe belong more to heaven than to earth. And yet, a role was preserved for Provence in that distribution of divine graces attached to the soil, a unique role, as if the last sign of the life of Jesus Christ among us.

On leaving Marseille in the direction of the Alps, one enters a valley that extends along the sea, unseen because high mountains hide its waves; another chain rises opposite that one. Thus confined between these two walls, the valley runs towards a rough amphitheater that seems to close the road, while a river bordered by trees glides effortlessly in long meadows and provides a thousand dwellings with its fruitfulness. Its name is as obscure as its waters. It guides the traveler, in a way, and, after expanding in a vast countryside, impeded by the mountains, it suddenly veers off to the left, plunges into closer passes, becomes a torrent. Finally, rising up between a maze of wooded peaks and bare summits, it finds its source in a peaceful plateau, crowned by an immense and solitary rock. A moment ago, we were in the middle of a rich and lively city, one of the queens of the Mediterranean. The rollers of the waves and the noise of men could be heard. From all points of the horizon, there arrived vessels, pushed less by the wind than by the treasures they carried. Now, everything has calmed down and at the same time remains unimportant. But with that peace, as with the bleakness of the desert, one could believe himself carried by mysterious routes to inaccessible secluded places of ancient Thebaide [a region of Egypt]. A few fallen walls can be seen in the middle of the plain, some houses on the fringes, behind a knoll. But these vestiges of life do not diminish the solemn reality of this place. The heart is aware that it is in a solitude wherein God is not a stranger.

In the center of the high and aligned rocks, looking like a curtain of stone, the eye discovers a dwelling that appears to be suspended there, and at his feet, a forest whose novelty surprises him. This is no longer the thin pine tree that perfumes Provence, nor the holm oak, nor any of the shade trees that the traveler met on the road. It would seem that by a strange marvel the North had planted there all the magnificence of its vegetation. It is the soil and the sky of the South with the forests of England. Close by, at two paces, on the sides of the mountain, is to be found the genuine nature of the country. This is the only exception. If you enter into it, immediately the forest envelops you in all its majesty, likened in its depths, its veils and its silences, to those holy woodlands that the ancients never profaned. There also, only the centuries have access; only the centuries had the right to fell old trunks and to rejuvenate their sap. Alone, they reigned and still reign, instruments of a respect that comes from higher up, and that adds to the reaction of sight that of thought.

Who passed by there? Who marked this section of land with such a powerful stamp? What is this rock? What is this forest? Finally, what is this land where everything seems to be bigger than we are?

Oh Marseille! You saw arrive the first resident of this mountain. You saw disembarking from a ship a frail creature who brought you a second visit from the East. The first one had given you your port, your walls, your name, even your existence. The second one gave you even better; it entrusted to you living relics of the life of Jesus Christ, souls that He had loved the most tenderly on earth, and, so to speak, the final testament of the friendship of a God. It was from the height of His cross that Jesus Christ entrusted his mother to the Apostle John. For you, it was from the height of his resurrection, between the scattered shadows of death and the brilliant lights of eternal life, that Jesus chose you as the tested haven for his dearest friends. Must they be named for you? Must you be told who they were? No, your memory was always faithful to them, your history speaks to you of them, your walls have mixed tradition to the memories of your early faith. The sacred dawn of your Christianity is the very tomb where you venerate in your apostles the friends of Jesus.

It was Lazarus, the man brought back to life in Bethany; it was Martha, his sister, who saw him come out of his burial place, and who believed in the power of the Son of man, even before it was made manifest. It was another woman, sister to both of them, yet even more illustrious, loved more greatly, and worthy of it, the one about whom it was said: *Many sins are forgiven her because she has loved much.* She was the first to see and to touch Jesus on the morning of his resurrection, because she was the first in His heart — a heart that was nonetheless wounded by a love that embraced all souls up to death.

I am writing about this woman. Praised throughout the world by the Gospel, she has no need of a mortal pen to reanimate in the shadows of the 19th century the glory of those days. No other name besides hers has resisted indifference because sin itself has opened roads for her in the admiration of men, and virtue opened up another route in the generation of spotless hearts. Mary Magdalene touches both sides of our life: the sinner anoints us with her tears, the saint anoints us with her tenderness. One soothes our wounds at the feet of Christ, the other tests us with the raptures of His ascension. But if Mary Magdalene has no need of being praised by a mouth other than God's, we can still find joy in something useless to her, and offer her some incense that will return to us as a blessing.

This is our hope. Perhaps also the ruins of the *Sainte-Baume* [the grotto where she dwelt] will thrill at our voice, and Provence, moved by a lack of restraint that reveals its piety, might find once again for such a lofty veneration the love of its ancestors and the generosity of its princes.

CHAPTER 1

Friendship in Jesus Christ

Friendship is the most perfect of man's feelings because it is the most free, the most untainted, and the deepest. In the relationships of filial piety and of maternal love, the child did not choose his father or his mother; he was born of them without him. As soon as his heart opens up with his youth, he knows more and more the need to love by an act that provides it and which he wants. If the parents, too wide awake of what is missing in the affection of the best child, struggle to win him over by weakness that brings them close to infancy, usually they simply set themselves up for more ingratitude. Moreover, if, being jealous of the holy authority that age and reason grant them, they exercise it with the energy of a tenderness that does not forget its duty, the child — more docile, it is true, better behaved, better taught about his place — is not prevented from imagining a fear, however filial it be, that will avert the notion of a misleading equality.

Barely a man, even before he becomes one, the child of the most lovable mother aspires to separate himself from her and so verify the words of Scripture, so gentle and so terrifying at the same time: *Man will leave his father and mother, and attach himself to his wife*. There, at least, will he find that freedom of choice which is one of the conditions of love? Far from it. A thousand pressing circumstances show to man the companion of his life. Birth, fortune, chance, dictate laws at the moment when his heart alone ought to command; and so, a victim crowned with bitter roses, he approaches the altar to promise everything but to give much less. How many marriages there are where love is absent! How many domestic hearts have for their household gods only a poorly disguised indifference. If these two souls have really talked to each other, if the rare spark of a common affection has brightened the two who vow, how many traps there are in that happiness and how many causes of its untimely decay.

Conjugal love, the strongest of all while it lasts, is nonetheless a weakness that arises from its very enthusiasm. The feelings are not strangers to it. The beauty of the body is its principal nourishment, and that beauty, while it lasts, is not guaranteed to keep its control over the heart that it captivated. All too often, while the world still admires it, it lost the joy of its rule, and the crowd offers wishes that fall over a secret and painful ruin. That lovely head no longer speaks to the one who had admired it. An unknown abandon, one that cannot even be blamed, follows the elation of a devotion that had promised itself timelessness. If the charm itself is prolonged as much as its cause, that very cause soon begins to wither. Youth, which is a necessary element of evident beauty, rushes to its end; in vain does skill struggle against a decline that is inevitable. The spouse wishes to delude himself, and he does that for a while. But the time comes when this is no longer possible; and the love that held by a delicate thread these traits and appearances, little by little disappears while it seeks again what it loved yesterday.

Friendship, when it is genuine, is not readily affected by these reversals of fortune. Based on the beauty of the soul, it arises from regions more liberal, purer, and deeper than any other affection. It is not the breast of a woman bent over a cradle that gives it day; it does not have as its opening a contract that ties interests together, and that approves an altar whose fire contains embers. It comes from man by an act of supreme freedom; and this freedom remains to the end, without the law of man or the law of God ever authorizing the decisions. Friendship lives by itself and by itself alone; free in its origins, it remains so during its course. Its sustenance is an immaterial openness between two souls, a mysterious resemblance between the invisible beauty of both, a beauty that the senses can perceive in the revelation of the countenance, but that the outpouring of a confidence which grows on its own manifests even more surely. Finally, light appears, without shadows and without limits, at which time the friendship becomes the joint possession of two wills, of two virtues, of two beings always free to separate but that never do. Age could not weaken such dealings, because the soul has no age. Superior to time, it inhabits the eternal place of spirits; fully attached to the body that it animates, it does not notice — if it so chooses — its weaknesses and stains. And yet, by an admirable privilege, time confirms friendship. As events take place in the lives of two friends, their loyalty grows stronger though trials. They appreciate better the unity of their feelings that a shock could have destroyed or shaken. Like two rocks overhanging similar waves and showing them unwavering resistance, so do they notice the flow of years vainly attack the unchanging harmony of their hearts. One must be alive to be sure of being loved.

But is this not simply a dream? Is friendship nothing else but a sublime and consoling word? There are mothers who love their sons; there are wives who love their husbands. These are imperfect ties, but they do exist. Does friendship exist? Is it not a flower of youth that withers before spring? Is it not one of those golden clouds that appear at daybreak and never see the night?

For a long while, I thought that youth was the age of friendship, and that friendship itself was like the gracious introduction to all our affections. I was mistaken. Youth is too unsteady for friendship; it is not yet solidly based in its thoughts or its desires, and, in giving itself, can offer no more than hope. On the other hand, maturity is too dispassionate for such a noble sentiment; there are too many interests that preoccupy it and tie it down. Youth lacks that generous freedom of a being that does not yet belong to the world, as well as a certain naiveté that believes, an enthusiasm which surrenders itself, an independence that fears nothing of life. Must I therefore suppress the very title of this chapter and include friendship among the dreams of Adam's posterity? No! The Gospel prevents me, as does my own history. No doubt I have left on the road, like profane remains, many affections that had enchanted me. I saw perish in my heart the immaterial beauty of more than one beloved soul. And yet, it would be as difficult for me to disbelieve in friendship as to disbelieve in religion. I believe in the fondness of men as I believe in the goodness of God. Man deceives, God never deceives; therein lies the difference between them. Man does not always deceive; in this is to be found his resemblance to God. Creature weak and fallible, his friendship is worth all the more in that he conceives it and carries it in a more fragile vessel. He loves sincerely in a spirit subject to egoism; he loves purely in a corrupt flesh; he loves eternally on a day that will end. This I believe and this I know. To this, youth brings more promptness in sympathy, maturity, more constancy, old age more impartiality and depth. Besides, neither rank, nor fortune, nor anything that separates men has any influence here. We have seen kings love one of their subjects, slaves attach themselves to their masters. Friendship is born from one soul into another soul; and the soul has value only in itself. Once we meet there, everything else disappears. Just as on that one day, and much better, when we will meet each other in God, the universe will be for us but a forgotten spectacle. But it is difficult to meet each other in a place as far away as the soul, so hidden behind the ocean that surrounds it, and under the clouds that cover it. Scripture says of God that he inhabits *inaccessible light*; one can say that the soul inhabits an impenetrable darkness. We believe we touched it, but the hand that sought it had barely caught the hem of its clothing. It draws back and leaves just as we believe ourselves sure of having taken it — now a snake, then a fearful dove, a flame or an icicle, a torrent or a peaceful lake — and always, whatever its form or image, the trial wherein we most come to grief, and the port where we enter the least. Friendship, then, is a rare and divine entity, the sure sign of a great soul and the highest visible reward attached to virtue.

Moreover, it could not be a stranger to Christianity, that raised up souls and created so many virtues. When two Christian spouses, for example, found in their faith the principle of their fidelity, Jesus Christ, who blessed their love, did not promise it eternal duration. Nothing that is intangible is immortal. But as the ardors of the blood weaken at the same time as beauty fades, that very fact, instead of being a sign of decline, is the forerunner of progress. The soul does not detach itself because the body has lost its ties;

confidence, esteem, respect, the habit of an intimate and reciprocal affection, maintain in hearts the home of an affection that strengthens itself while purifying itself. Tenderness survives under a different form. It is no longer the earthly emotion of other times but the divine thrill of spirits helped by the remembrance of a youth that was unsullied at the same time as it was charming. The crown of virgins descends from the sacred heights of Christian marriage to the brow of spouses; together, they sing a hymn that even death cannot silence, because eternity lends them that hymn here below, and grants it to them in the bosom of God. Instead of that terrible helplessness to which the blemished flesh condemns the living heart, friendship gets up from the nuptial bed that has grown cold like a lily perfumed by a love that is no longer there. Old age itself, bathed in the perfume that transfigures it, bows toward the grave like those century-old trees which kept for their final years their most beautiful flowers and their best fruits. In Christianity, friendship is the term and the supreme reward of conjugal love.

Moreover, friendship is also that for the virtues of youth. When a young man, helped by the all-powerful grace that comes from Christ, controls his passions under the yoke of chastity, he experiences in his heart an expansion proportionately equal to the reserve of his senses. Then, the need to love, which is the basis of our nature, appears to him by a naive enthusiasm that leads him to pour himself out into a fervent and restrained soul like his. He does not long seek in vain its apparition. It offers itself to him naturally, like every plant that grows in appropriate soil. Sympathy refuses itself only to him who does not inspire it, but he who does inspire it carries within himself generous leaven. Every untainted heart has it, and consequently, every untainted heart attracts to itself, at whatever age. But more so during youth! How much more so when the brow is decorated with all the graces that soften, and which virtue brightens with that other beauty which pleases God himself! Thus did David appear to Jonathan on the day when he entered the tent of Saul holding the head of the giant in his right hand, and whose origin the king asked about. David answered: "I am the son of your servant Isaiah, of Bethlehem." Immediately, said Scripture, *Jonathan attached himself to the soul of David, and Jonathan loved him like his own soul* (I Kings18:1). Strange effect from a single glance! Just a while before, David was watching the flock of his father, while Jonathan was on the threshold of the throne: in an instant, the distance is erased. The shepherd and the prince, in the words of the Scriptures, are but one soul. This is because in the young man, still pale from the weaknesses of childhood, yet holding in a manly hand the bloody head of a vanquished enemy, Jonathan saw the hero, and David, on seeing the son of his king, bending toward him with no jealousy of his victory and no pride of rank, recognized in that generous movement a heart able to love, and worthy, consequently, of being loved.

Among the ancients, neither conjugal love nor the charm of youth could produce that Christian friendship whose traits we have just sketched. The female was brought too low to hold herself up in an attachment to the male by the sole effect of acquired confidence and prompt respect; her influence fell along with her beauty, and it was rare that she could survive by herself in more perfect feelings. However magnificent and touching in Christianity, old age brought her, along with the blemishes of time, only the wrong of abandonment. She was happy when there remained a place for her in the family residence, under the protection of a law less harsh than the heart of her spouse.

As for the young man of antiquity, too little chaste to be loved, in the rapture of his passions, whatever they were, he felt little of the outpourings of blameless enthusiasm. He loved with his senses much more than with his soul; even if the word friendship had been known by him — because man never completely ignored nor corrupted his nature — nonetheless he lacked, except perhaps in rare cases, the blow of a weapon that causes to flow within us the source of unblemished affections. Jesus Christ was not the first father of friendship among men; it existed in the earthly paradise when Adam and Eve, still clothed with their innocence as with a veil, walked together under the eye of God, in love with one another from a feeling whose tenderness was equal to purity. But that was just for one day, perhaps for an hour. Soon, the flesh, frightened about itself, enveloped itself in gloomy shadows, and man no longer loved as he had loved before. And yet, he brought from this first love, in the degradation of his exile, a memory that followed him everywhere. When the Son of God came to save him, neither of them was surprised that the Gospel was a book of love, and love the book of salvation. Jesus Christ did not create tenderness or purity, those two divine qualities by which our heart was molded; but He restored them to us. He loved in a way no longer found. In the many friendships whose secret He revealed to us, I wish to indicate one of which no trace existed before him.

Jesus Christ loved souls and transmitted this love to us, a love that is the very foundation of Christianity. No true Christian, no living Christian can be without a portion of this love that circulates in our veins like the very blood of Christ. As soon as we love — whether in youth or in maturity, as father or as spouse, as son or as friend — we wish to save the soul that we love, which is to say, to give it, at the price of our own life, truth in faith, virtue in grace, peace in redemption — finally, God, God known, God loved, God served. In this is the love of souls that is super-added to all others, and which, far from destroying them, raises them up and transforms them to the point of making something divine, all natural that they be by themselves. Now it happens that love of souls leads to friendship.

When one is near a poor fallen creature, the instrument of light that reveals to him his fall and restores its elevation, that sublime healing from a death that was supposed to be eternal, sometimes inspires in both souls an undefinable attraction born of happiness given and happiness received. If natural sympathy adds itself to the change that comes from higher up, from all those divine chance happenings in similar hearts there arises an attachment that would have no name on earth were it not for Jesus Christ to have told His disciples: *I call you friends.* It is therefore FRIENDSHIP. This is the friendship such as God become man and dying for His friends could conceive of it. But more, among those souls with whom Jesus Christ lived and died, there were those who were the object of preference. He loved them all, but He loved some more than others. In this, in this world, is to be found the summit of human and divine affections. Nothing had prepared the world for this, and the world will never see but a dim picture of it in the holiest and most celestial friendships.

CHAPTER II

Some friendships of Jesus in Bethany

St. John is the evangelist of the divinity of Jesus Christ. No one else understood Him better; no one repeated more faithfully what the Son of Man affirmed about the Son of God, and saw from up close what he had heard less distantly. On reading him, one is surprised that Arianism could have been possible, so much that at each step, there bursts the coeternal union of the Word with God, of the Son with the Father. But by another privilege, St. John is also the evangelist of the heart of Jesus Christ. As a preferred object himself, no one has expressed better how much he loved Him, no one reported the most touching and best imprinted features in that admirable history of which he is one of the four authors.

Here is how St. John opens the eleventh chapter of his Gospel:

"There was a man called Lazarus who was ill in Bethany, in the town of Mary and Martha, her sister.

"This Mary was the one who anointed the Savior with perfume and wiped his feet with her hair, and it was her brother Lazarus who was ill.

"The two sisters sent a message to Jesus, to tell him: "Lord, the one you loved is ill.""

"On hearing this, Jesus said to his disciples: 'This illness is not to death, but for the glory of God, so that the Son of God be glorified by it.'

"Now Jesus loved Martha and her sister Mary, as well as Lazarus. And even when he had learned that Lazarus was ill, he remained two days in the same place. Then he told his disciples: 'Let us go to Judea again.'

'His disciples said to him: 'Master, the Jews seek to stone you, and you want to go back there?' Jesus replied: 'Are there not twelve hours in a day? If someone walks during the day, he does not trip because he sees the light of this world; but if he walks at night, he trips because he does not have the light in him.' "

This is what he told them, then he added: 'Lazarus, our friend, is sleeping; but I will waken him from his sleep.' His disciples said to him: 'Lord, since he sleeps, he will be saved.' Now Jesus had spoken of death, but they understood it as ordinary sleep. And so, he told them openly: 'Lazarus is dead.

" 'And I rejoice because of you, so that you may believe, since I was not there; but let us go to him.' Then Thomas, called Didymus [the Twin], told the other disciples: 'Let us also go, so as to die with him.' Jesus then set out; He arrived after Lazarus had been four days in the tomb.

"Now Bethany was near Jerusalem, at a distance of about fifteen stadia. And many Jews had come to Martha and Mary to console them after the death of their brother. As soon as Martha heard of Jesus' arrival, she ran to meet him; as for Mary, she remained seated in the house.

"Martha then told Jesus : 'Lord, if you had been here, my brother would not have died. But I know that all you will ask of God, God will grant you.' Jesus told her: "Your brother will rise.'

"Martha said to him, 'I know that he will rise at the resurrection, on the last day.' Jesus said to her: 'I am the resurrection and the life; he who believes in me will live, though he be dead. Whoever lives and believes in me will not die forever. Do you believe that?' She replied: 'Yes, Lord, I believe that you are the Christ, Son of the living God, who has come into this world.'

"And after having said that, she left. Calling Mary, her sister, she told her in a low voice, "The Master is there and is asking for you.' Having heard this, Mary immediately got up and went to him. For Jesus had not yet entered the town, and had remained where Martha had met him. Now the Jews who had come with her to the house and were consoling her, seeing that she had gotten up and left quickly, followed her, saying: 'She is going to the tomb, there to weep.'

"But Mary, having arrived at the place where Jesus was, and seeing him, fell at his feet and said to him: 'Lord, if you had been here, my brother would not have died.' Jesus, seeing that she was weeping, as were the Jews who had come with her, shuddered in his mind and was himself troubled. He said: 'Where have you placed him?' They said, 'Lord, come and see.' And Jesus wept.

"The Jews said among themselves: 'See how

much he loved him.' But some said to themselves:

" 'Is he not the one who opened the eyes of a man born blind? Could he not have done something so that this one not die?' Now Jesus, trembling a second time, came to the tomb, which was a cave, with a stone closing it.

"Jesus said: 'remove the stone.' Martha, sister of the dead man, told him: 'Lord, there is already an odor, for he has been dead for four days.' Jesus said to her: 'ave I not told you that, if you believed, you would see the glory of God?' The stone was then removed, and Jesus. His eyes turned toward heaven, said: "Father, I give you thanks that you have heard me.

" 'I know, it is true, that you always hear me, but I said this for the people who surround me, so that they may believe that you sent me.' Having said this, he cried out in a loud voice: 'Lazarus, come out.' Immediately, the one who was dead appeared, feet and hands bound by bands, his face covered with a shroud. Jesus said to them: 'Untie him, and let him go.' "

I do not know what others may think; as for me, were there only this page in the Gospel, I would believe in the divinity of Jesus Christ. Try as I might to remember all that I read, I know of nothing else wherein truth asserts itself with such evident power. There is no word therein that does not convey to the depths of man the conviction that God alone could have acted in this way and have it written about in this way. As a display of friendship, nothing like it exists in any century and in any language. Tenderness overflows in this story, and yet you could say it was not expressed. It lies completely in feelings and, in always being aware of it, it can be understood by these simple words: *And Jesus wept.* Jesus was not to weep during his passion; He did not weep when an apostle gave Him the kiss of betrayal, nor when St. Peter denied Him in fear of a servant woman, nor when He saw at the foot of the cross, His mother and His dearest friends. It was the supernatural hour of our redemption; the divinity of the Just Man, who was redeeming us by pain, could not make itself visible except by influence and by majesty. But on the eve of this moment, when Christ, still free, lived among us with our life, He could not refuse at the tomb of a friend the weakness of compassion. He trembled, He was troubled, and finally, like one of us, He wept. What holy shudders, blessed disorder, precious tears, that prove to us that our God is sensitive like us, and allows us to weep also on the day of our joys and of our friendships!

Thus, Jesus had in Bethany a complete family of friends. It was there that, coming from Jerusalem — the city where He was to complete His sacrifice — He rested from the weariness of preaching and the painful outlook of the future. There, pure and devoted hearts, friends, were to be found; there, this incomparable good of an affection shielded from everything. Moreover, it was from Bethany that he set out for this triumphal entry into Jerusalem; it was at the sight of Bethany, his face turned to its walls, on the East, that he ascended to heaven, almost at an equal distance from Calvary where he died to the house where he had been loved the most. Even today, when the traveler coming from Jerusalem has passed the torrent of Kedron and climbed the Mount of Olives, he discovers on the eastern slope of those hills some hovels strewn with ruins. A pointed finger shows him, among the ruins, three points barely noticeable among formless remnants. "There," he is told, "was the house of Lazarus; there, that of Martha; and there that of Mary Magdalene." The memory of centuries was stronger than the destruction of barbarity, and the names of the friends of Jesus, outlasting the scattered stones, still strike with a stirring tone this indifferent silence. On the other side, and from the same place where he is standing, the traveler discovers Jerusalem lying in the evening sunshine, sad, pensive, having only one tomb for glory, but it is the tomb of its God! The thought and the eye of the Christian wander between these two spectacles of unlike desolation. Here, nothing left but the name; there, still one city, but what a city! Jesus did not wish to leave so close to it the residence and the tomb of His friends. He took everything away with his ascension, and plunging Bethany beyond the seas, he prepared for those who loved him, on shores forever Christian, an everlasting hospitality.

But if, by restoring in thought those vanished homes, we enter them piously, following the

Master; if we sit at the evening dinner with Jesus, Lazarus, Martha, and Mary, we will perhaps ask ourselves to whom of these favored hosts did the heart of Jesus give himself the most? Indeed, within preferences there are preferences, so deep is love, with a boundless hierarchy. Can we penetrate this mystery? Are we allowed to look into it with the Gospel, and bring to it the holy curiosity of an undefiled devotion? I do believe so. We can never know too much about where the heart of the Master was, so that we might know whom we ought to love more with Him and after Him. If the Christian searches the dust for the footprints of the Savior, how much more ought he to search the Gospel for traces of His attachments. I will therefore look for them. As a voyager with memories of Bethany, I can cross the threshold and see what is going on, hear all that is being said, and answer myself when I ask: Who, then, was the most beloved?

Was it Lazarus? There is only this brief word about him, a word common to Martha and to Mary: *Jesus loved Lazarus.* And this other word, which is personal to him: *Lazarus our friend, sleeps.* And this final word: *Lazarus, come out.*

As for Martha, she was the first to know that Jesus had arrived, she is the first to run to Him, the first to say to Him: *Lord, if you had been here, my brother would not have died.* But when the Savior answered her: *Your brother will rise,* she was not overcome by a light that would make her understand the sovereign thought of the Son of God. Her faith hesitates, Jesus has to tell her: *I am the resurrection and life; do you believe that?* Then, despite these repeated affirmations, when the Lord orders that the stone be removed from the tomb, she cannot help but remark that the dead man has been there for four days. Once again, the Lord has to reproach her: *Have I not told you that you would see the glory of God?*

Mary is in less of a hurry than Martha. First of all, she does not know that Jesus has arrived, so she remains sitting in the house, until Martha comes to tell her softly: *The Master is there, and he calls for you.* It is Jesus who calls Mary. He does not want what He has decided to take place far from her eyes. As for her, as soon as she learns of the coming of the Master, she runs to Him and falls at his feet. Martha had remained standing, Mary falls to the feet of the one she loves. Her words are the same as those of her sister: *Lord, if you had been here, my brother would not have died.* But Jesus does not respond, nor does He ask her for an act of faith. He knows she believes. The sight of her tears touched Him, and He Himself weeps. Up to that point, He had maintained control over Himself; in the presence of Mary His weakness breaks out. He shudders, He becomes troubled, He weeps. *And Jesus wept.*

And so there was in Mary a deeper humility, a livelier faith, a stronger reaction on the heart of Jesus. She was loved with a preference that her virtues revealed, because they were at the same time the effect and the cause of her love for the Son of God. This judgment is confirmed by a famous passage in the Gospel of St. Luke, in his tenth chapter. "Now, it happened that while Jesus was on a trip, he entered a certain town; a woman named Martha received him in her home. She had a sister named Mary, who, keeping herself at the feet of the Lord, listened to His words. As for Martha, she was busy with all kinds of matters regarding serving; standing before the Lord, she told Him: 'Lord, are you not anxious that my sister leaves me to serve alone? Tell her to help me.' Answering, the Lord told her: 'Martha, Martha, you are preoccupied and troubled by many things. Only one thing is necessary. Mary has chosen the better part that will not be taken from her.' " What is that better part, if not a greater love for Our Lord, earned by a more perfect response? Martha was serving, Mary remained silent. Between these two reactions, so differently expressed, it is impossible to hesitate. On declaring that Mary's was preferable, Jesus necessarily was characterizing her as preferred, and preferred with the promise that the better part would remain with her unceasingly.

But who was that Mary, who came to the love of Christ after completely setting aside all that was not the gaze and the meditation? St. John was careful to tell us as soon as the second verse of his story. He had barely named Mary when he interrupted himself to tell us: *This was the Mary who had anointed the Lord with a perfume and wiped his feet with her hair.* Evidently, the apostle attached great value in having us know this, and to have us learn it by an action that does not allow us to confuse her with any other woman of the Gospel. If another had *anointed the Lord with perfume and wiped his feet with her hair*, that action no longer applicable to a single person would have ceased identifying clearly that this was Mary of Bethany. Now St. John wished to identify her clearly, and he wished to do this because the action he used to distinguish her from all other creatures was an extraordinary act, unique, sublime in his eyes and worthy of eternal memory. Many women followed Jesus and served him; many bore him a love worthy of the Son of man and of the Son of God: of the Son of God by the chaste worship of supernatural tenderness, of the Son of Man by the cares they offered this sick nature that He had taken in our favor. But only one among many had taken the step of anointing him with perfume and drying his dampened feet with the towel of her hair. This last situation reveals a single soul. There are some things that can be repeated by the soul that conceived them, but cannot be imitated by another. Twice did a woman fall at the feet of the Savior; twice a woman poured on them the liquid of an expensive perfume and wiped them with her hair. But even when the Gospel would not name her, when even tradition remained silent, we could be sure that this was the case of a single inspiration, and that if the anointing was two-fold, there was only one heart to think of this and only one hand to do it, just as there was but one God to receive it.

This is how the earliest and the latest centuries understood matters. Mary of Bethany, sister of Lazarus and of Martha, is the only woman who twice anointed the feet of the Savior and dried them with her hair. At the second anointing that preceded the death of the Son of God by three days, the evangelist identifies her by her name and by the place where the scene was enacted. In the first, which signaled the beginning of the public ministry of Jesus Christ, Mary was not named; we will see why, and I have just said how the silence was repaired.

CHAPTER III

The first anointing of Jesus by Mary of Bethany, aka Mary Magdalene

Jesus Christ had begun his public ministry. It was not to last long. From the first moment, we see around him three kinds of persons: first of all, simple disciples, men converted by his word, seeing him and treating him as Savior of the world; then, among them, twelve apostles chosen to be the foundation of the spiritual society of which their master would eternally be the life; and finally, among those apostles and disciples, some souls destined to be the friends and comforters of God made man. No doubt, all of them were united to Him by bonds of charity — except for a traitor and some defectors — and loved him with a sincere love that Jesus Christ granted to all of them, but greater for His apostles, allowing Him to say to them: *I call you my friends.* Yet it is clear, when reading the Gospel, that the apostles themselves, all chosen as they were and holding first place in the work of redemption, were not, by the privilege of their future, the dearest of the heart that had called them. Since he wished to have a mother, Jesus, the image of our life, had also wished to have friends who were such by another title than their duty, the title of a benevolence independent of any other principle than itself. St. John was one of them, and he himself, in his Gospel, distinguishes himself from the others by these beautiful words of grace and simplicity: *The disciple whom Jesus loved.*

We do not find in the Gospel the original causes of this preference for St. John. He was he son of a fisherman of Galilee, and had a brother named James. One day, as they were repairing their nets aboard a boat, Jesus saw them and called them. Immediately, says the Gospel, they left their nets and followed him (*Mt* 4:20). This is all we know about the origins of a friendship that made John an apostle, an evangelist, a martyr, the last of the prophets. But this was not the case with Mary, the sister of Lazarus and of Martha. Here is the scene in which she appears to us for the first time, at the feet of him who was to make of her the most illustrious of women, with only one exception.

The story is from St. Luke in his chapter seven.

A Pharisee had invited Jesus to dinner with him. Jesus entered the house of the Pharisee, approached the table, at which he halfway reclined. And there came a woman, a sinner in the city, who on having learned that he would be at table in the house of the Pharisee, went there with an alabaster jar filled with perfume. Remaining in the background, along his feet, she began to water his feet with her tears and drying them with her hair; she kissed his feet and anointed them with the perfume. Seeing this, the Pharisee who had invited Jesus, began to say to himself: If he were a prophet, he would certainly know what kind of woman it was that touched him and that she was a sinner. Jesus, answering his thought, said to him: "Simon, I have something to tell you." And Simon replied: "Speak, Lord." "A money lender had two debtors, one who owed five hundred *denarii*, the other fifty.

"Now, neither of them having the means to pay him back, he forgave both of them their debt. Which of the two loved him the more?" Simon replied: "I think it is the one to whom he gave the most." And Jesus answered: "You have judged correctly." Turning toward the woman, he said to Simon: "You see this woman? I entered your house and you did not wash my feet with water; but she washed them with her tears, and dried them with her hair. You did not give me a kiss; but since she entered, she has not stopped kissing my feet. You did not anoint my head with oil, but she anointed my feet with perfume. This is why I tell you: Many sins have been forgiven her because she has loved much; the one who is forgiven less is the one who has loved less." Then He said to the woman: "Your sins are forgiven." Those who were at table with Him began to say to each other: "Who is this who forgives sin?" Now Jesus said to the woman: "Your faith has saved you. Go in peace."

Few pages of the Gospel have given to the hearts of men so penetrating a feature, and without a doubt no friendship on earth ever started

34

like this one. From the most profound depths that a person of her sex could fall, a woman raises her eyes to divine purity and does not despair of the beauty of her soul. Still a sinner, she has recognized God in the flesh of the Son of man, and, filled with shame, she has the thought of approaching Him. She takes a precious perfume in an alabaster jar, symbol of light. Perhaps this was the jar from which up to that point she had sought relief from her criminal attractions, and this, the perfume that she had intended for another use, perhaps she had sought for herself an increase of her shameful pleasures. She had profaned everything and was able to present to God only ruins. Moreover, she entered without uttering a word, and would leave in the same way. Repentant, she will not accuse herself before him who knows everything. Forgiven, she will not express any feeling of gratitude. The entire mystery lies in her heart; her silence, which is an act of faith and of humility, is also the last effort of a soul that overflows and can do no more. It was the custom of the voluptuous East to perfume one's head and it was respect to touch a man in this way with an anointing on the top of his beauty. Mary knew this more than anyone else and often, during the days of her faults, she had thus honored the slaves of her seduction. Thus, she was far from approaching the blessed head of the Savior, like a servant used to the most lowly functions; instead, she bends toward his feet, and at first, without touching them, she waters them with her tears. Never, since the beginning of the world, had such tears fallen on the feet of a man. One might have admired them out of fear or out of love; one could have washed them with perfumed waters, and, in the centuries of primitive hospitality some daughters of kings would not have scorned offering this tribute to the weariness of the stranger. But this was the first time that repentance sat in silence at the feet of a man and poured out tears capable of redeeming a life.

While weeping and without waiting for a word of encouragement that would not come, Mary let fall the hair around her head, and, using her shock of hair as a magnificent instrument of her repentance, she wiped with its humbled silk the tears she had shed. It was also the first time that a woman condemned, or rather consecrated, her hair to this ministry of tenderness and atonement. We had seen some women cut their hair as a sign of mourning; others offer it as a sign of homage at the altar of some divinity or other. But nowhere does history, which recorded all that was unusual in the movements of man, show us that repentance and sin together created so touching a picture of themselves. History struck the disciple with love, instructed as he was in the internal secrets of the burnt offering. In a wish to transmit to future centuries the particulars about Mary, history found no better way to make this known than to say of her: *It was this Mary who anointed the Lord with perfume and who dried his feet with her hair.*

Having done this, the sinful woman became bolder. She brought her dishonored lips to the feet of the Savior, covered them with kisses that gave the impression of all the ones she had given and those she had received. On contact with this more than virginal flesh, the last vapors of old memories vanished. The un-atonable stains disappeared, and this transfigured mouth breathed only the brisk air of holiness. Only then, and to complete all mystery of repentance by love, she opens the alabaster jar that contains along with the perfume pleasing images of immortality, pours it over the feet of the Savior, over the tears and the kisses with which she had covered them. Her purified hands no longer feared to touch and anoint the Son of God. The house was filled with the virtue that comes from the fragile and immortal jar, from the alabaster and from the heart.

Who would believe it? Man did not understand this spectacle; he understood neither repentance, nor expiation, nor love, nor pardon. His only thought was a doubt about the God who had just given so impressive a revelation of his presence.

It was then that was opened the sublime dialogue between Jesus Christ and the Pharisee with the words: *Simon, I have something to tell you*, and that ends with these: *Many sins have been forgiven her because she has loved much.* Ah! It was not in vain that posterity heard them. It was not in vain that such actions and such expressions enlightened our poor nature. No, you chaste tears of the converted sinful woman, hair flowing over the feet of the Savior, sweet and bitter tears of repentance, perfume spread on the unsullied flesh of the God-Man; no, you were not without benefit! Generations followed the tracks of these unutterable dealings between sin and Justice, between eternal death and eternal life. Other Marys got up from the bed of vice; from century to century, they approached the still damp feet of the Savior of men; they wept in turn, and in turn they attached to them the bonds of their hair. They offered modest kisses, acquired from remorse, and poured the perfume remaining in the bottom of the jar where the first Mary had left it. The world saw it; the enemy of purity that resisted could not refuse its admiration of a purity that was reborn from its ashes. And yet, blind as he is, he understood why Jesus, in wishing to choose some friends for Himself on the earth, had called the sinful woman after having chosen the chastity of St. John — why He granted pardon to him who had pronounced on the fallen woman this adorable absolution: *Many sins have been forgiven her because she has loved much.* O my God, you are God because your words have created virtue and your friendship for a sinful woman created some saints.

This was the first anointing of Jesus by Mary of Bethany. It probably took place in Bethany itself, because the evangelist saint Luke, the only

one to report it, states expressly that the scene
took place in the house and at the table of a
Pharisee called Simon. Now, according St.
Matthew and St. Mark, the second anointing,
about which we will speak shortly, took place in
Bethany, in the house and at the table of Simon
the leper; St. John adds that Lazarus was among
the guests and that Martha was serving them. This
resemblance between Simon the Pharisee and
Simon the leper in two events that are
comparable, and which nonetheless differ in time
and circumstance, leads us to think that both
anointings took place at the home of the same
Simon, linked as a neighbor with the family of
Lazarus and of Martha, and consequently, in
Bethany. At the time of the first anointing, Mary
was still a sinner, and it was her conversion that
introduced Jesus to the acquaintanceship of
Lazarus and his relatives. From that time on,
Bethany became for the Lord a haven of
tenderness and of peace, the only place that seems
to have inspired him, by his return visits, to create
memories and to leave there feelings of
preference.

I have given the sister of Lazarus and of
Martha, the divine friend of Jesus Christ, the
name Mary of Bethany. And yet, nowhere in the
Gospel is she called that. The Gospel of St. John,
in the two famous chapters on the resurrection of
Lazarus and of the final anointing, identifies her
only by the links with Lazarus and Martha. She is
always there, that Mary, sister of Martha and of

Lazarus. Besides, everywhere else she seems to disappear. She is not found under the designation of family, either at the foot of the cross, or at the tomb of the Savior, at the resurrection, or anywhere else. This woman, a moment ago so exalted, you will shortly see anointing the feet of Jesus for a second time, two days before his passion. To vindicate her from the jealousies of which she is the object, Jesus will say: *Everywhere this Gospel will be preached, in all the world, what she has just done will be repeated in her honor.* (Mt 26:13) Then the woman disappears. Jesus still spoke of her and of the expensive perfume she had showered over him: *Leave her alone; may she be free to preserve it for the day of my burial.* (Jn 12:7) Nonetheless on the day foreseen for his burial, the sister of Martha and Lazarus does not show up. At Bethany, she is everything; outside of Bethany, she is nothing.

Evidently, that is not possible. Mary of Bethany has a name that ought to be extolled, a name spread on all the pages of the Gospel. If at the events in Bethany it is not said, it is because in that place, the very place pointed her out and named her so there be no mistake.

The Gospel knows only two Marys besides the Mother of God: Mary Magdalene, whom from whom St. Luke says that the Savior had expelled seven demons (Lk 8:2), and Mary, sister of the Most Holy Virgin, sometime called Mary of Cleophas, from the name of her husband, and as

Mary of James and Joseph, the names of her children. This is why St. Matthew, in speaking of the women who were present at the burial of the Lord, says very simply, not to mislead anyone: *There were also Mary Magdalene and the other Mary* (Mt 27:61) And later, on the morning of the resurrection: *Mary Magdalenee and the other Mary came to visit the tomb.*(Mt 28:1) If, outside of Mary Magdalene and Mary, the sister of the most holy Virgin, there had been another Mary, sister of Martha and of Lazarus, it is clear that the language of the evangelist would have been inexact and even misleading. For him, and consequently for the entire evangelical world, there were in the matters of the Lord, after Mary his mother, only two other Marys; Mary of Bethany would necessarily have been one of the two: either Mary Magdalene, or Mary of Cleophas. But she was not Mary of Cleophas, sister of the most holy Virgin, and so she was Mary Magdalene.

This is also what tradition, the liturgy of the Church, and the most ancient monuments raised to the memory of Mary Magdalene affirm. Their language shows us in the unity of a one and only glory, the sinful woman weeping at the feet of Jesus an drying them with her hair, the sister of Lazarus, present at the reanimation of her brother, the faithful friend standing at the passion and the death of her beloved, following him to the grave, and deserving to be the first to witness the splendors of his resurrection. All partitioning of that glory is delusion, contrary to Scripture, to the memory of ages, to the piety of the saints, to the universal veneration that everywhere places before the eyes and in the soul, the image of the sole woman in whom were accomplished the most touching mysteries of repentance and of friendship.

Mary was called Magdalene, from the town of Magdala, near the shores of Lake Galilee, either because she was a native there, or that she had resided there for a long time. What is certain is that she lived in Galilee. Indeed, both St. Matthew and St. Mark expressly state that she was among the women who had followed Jesus from Galilee and who ministered him. (Mt 27:56; Mk 15:10) This is why some writers thought that the conversion happened in Magdala, and that Simon the Pharisee, in the house where the first anointing took place, was none other than Simon the leper, where the second one occurred. Be that as it may, Mary Magdalene, recovered from her errors, and during the intervals when she was not following Jesus, remained in Bethany, near her brother and her sister, and that the tradition of the area held that her house there was separate from that of Lazarus and that of Martha.

CHAPTER IV

The second anointing of Jesus by Mary Magdalene

Meanwhile, the hour was approaching when the Son of God was to begin the redemption of the world by the sacrifice of His life, and put to the test the loyalty of those whom He had chosen and loved to a marked degree. Six days before that Passover, that was to be the last of the ancient world and the first of the new, He came to Bethany; that day, the very evening before His triumphal entry into Jerusalem, a supper was prepared for him in the house of a distinguished person whom the Gospel called Simon the leper. Lazarus was among the guests, and Martha, active as always, was eagerly serving them. This was not the last and supernatural supper that would immediately precede the death of the Savior, and end with the institution of the Eucharist all those sources of grace that He had made to spout over the world. This was a dinner of friendship, the last meal before the solemn week of the passion that was to open on the following day. Jesus Christ had only six more days to live in his mortal life, and in a few hours, he would appear in Jerusalem as its king, while waiting to die there shortly thereafter as its God. St. John has clearly marked this moment of pause in Bethany, at the beginning of the sorrowful way of the Son of Man. *Six days before Easter,* said he, *Jesus came to Bethany to the place where Lazarus had died, whom He brought back to life, and a supper was prepared for Him there. Martha was serving and Lazarus was one of the guests reclining with Him. (Jn 12:1-2)*

Since Jesus Christ, the true Passover, died on a Friday shortly before the final hours of the day, one must conclude that the event in Bethany took place on Saturday evening. It was not held at the house of Lazarus or that of one of the two sisters, but in the house of Simon the leper. This choice at such a moment proved that Simon was a stranger neither to Jesus Christ nor to the family of Lazarus. It also confirms us in our thought that it was indeed the same Simon who had been a witness and an actor three years earlier, at the conversion of Mary Magdalene.

The latter was not named among the guests or the servants. Her tenderness, instructed by an even higher light, told her that this meal had the character of a farewell, and that extreme events were being played out. So she took from an alabaster jar, as at the first time — a costly perfume that St. John called spikenard — and entered the dining hall. This was no longer the woman in whom youth and beauty disguised poorly the shame of vice and who approached the feet of Jesus timidly, like a servant, to shed tears on them and to dry them. Three years of grace had passed before her eyes; it was holiness that enveloped her entire person in a divine radiance.

44

She entered, then, and breaking the alabaster jar she held in her hands, poured the perfume over the head of the Savior. Magdalene broke the jar because she understood that everything was over, no more would the Lord receive from the piety of men similar reverence. This movement of prophetic despair and love completed, Mary remembered her early vileness and, running to the feet of Jesus, poured on them with the shards of a jar the rest of the perfume that she wiped with her hair. But the Gospel no longer named her tears. She was to shed them one last time at another time and in another place. Here, power and serenity were appropriate; this was no longer the hour of forgiveness and it was not yet the hour of the tomb.

Unending distress of men! This time it is not the Pharisee who begins to doubt God because he sees Him touched by a sinful woman; it is the disciples themselves who are shocked to see a very costly perfume poured on the head of their Master, on that head that they will shortly see under a crown of thorns. *Of what good*, they whispered among themselves, *the loss of this perfume? It could have been sold for more than three hundred denarii and these given to the poor.* (Mk 14:4- 5) We recognize the weakness of our mind when faced with the mysteries of God. Jesus does not take offense for their lack of faith; he tells them graciously: *Leave her alone; why do you grieve her? It was a good work that she did for me; you will always have the poor among you, and when you choose, you could do good for them, but you will not always have me around. This woman did what she was able to do with what she had, and she has, in advance, anointed my body for burial. In truth, I tell you, everywhere this Gospel will be preached, in all the world, what she has just done will be repeated to her glory.* (Mk 14:6 *et seq.*)

We have said that the supper of Bethany was a meal of friendship; it was to end in betrayal. The Savior had barely finished his words in which he justified the piety of Mary Magdalene that the Gospel adds: *Then one of the twelve called Judas Iscariot, went to find the princes of the priests and asked them: "What will you give me for me to deliver him to you?" And they agreed with him for thirty pieces of silver.* (Mt 26:14-15)

CHAPTER V

From Mary Magdalene to the cross and the tomb of Jesus

There remained the cross and the tomb; this is where eternity awaited both God and man. The cross and the tomb still endure, but they look only on man. At the time of which I am speaking, it was altogether the noble concern of man, and the noble concern of God. Let us approach them both, and first of all the cross, as the center where eternal wisdom was pleased to connect for us light, love, and life. Then, the day after the acclamations of Jerusalem, the second day of the joys of Bethany, it was only a horrible instrument, a torment of pain and disgrace. It frightened the world, and He was the one to reassure it; it was cursed, and yet it was He who was to bless. But this transfiguration had not yet taken place, and the cross of Calvary, the cross of the Son of man, displayed on that day all its horror and its nakedness. Let us look at it, to determine whom we will find loyal to this meeting of heaven and earth.

God is not there, since the Son complained that His Father had abandoned him. The angel of the Garden of Olives was not there either; and when the crucified uttered the words: *I thirst*, it was not the invisible hand of a spirit that presented him the cup. Nothing of heaven appears yet. The air is calm, the sun glows with the splendors of the East; Mount Zion does not tremble; the temple lies peacefully, and the veil that covers the Holy of Holies has not moved — it is the hour of the world, and the world is present. Here are the executioners who have finished their work and were resting. Beside them, the Pharisees who have not completed theirs and look insultingly at the one who revealed the hypocrisy of their virtues. At a distance, the Roman guard and the centurion who commands it, eyes fixed, heart disturbed by a foreboding that haunts him, but that has not yet enlightened him. Finally, the passers-by who shake their heads and who, without further worry about the spectacle, speak heartily: *Come now! You who would destroy the temple of God and rebuild it in three days, save yourself.* [Mt 27:40) Everywhere abandonment, silence, outrage, blasphemy, and yet, here is the Son of God, the Savior of the world, the King of the centuries, the heir of all that has been made, He before whom every knee will bend, in heaven, on earth and in the nether world. Alas! Not one of his own family is there, and, among the living and the dead, will no one come to recognize Him and greet Him in the divinity of His misery?

But no! Not everyone was absent. If God is absent, by a decree of his wisdom and His justice if He struck with terror, by another decree, most of those who had loved his Son, yet there remained one group at the foot of the cross, and

His eyes, on looking down, recognized His mother; Mary of Cleophas, sister of his mother; Salome, mother of the children of Zebedee; Mary Magdalene; the apostle St. John; and a few faithful, but unnamed women, who used to follow him and minister to him. Here, at the foot of the cross, you had all the love of the world. And that was enough; it was enough for the Savior to recognize all those who had loved Him since His coming on earth, and all those who would one day love Him. He saw in his Mother, the virgin par excellence, all the assembly of virgins; in Mary of Cleophas and in Salome, the entire chorus of Christian mothers and spouses; in St. John, the representation of the apostles, of martyrs, of prophets, of young men vowed to chastity, and of men drawing from faith the supernatural dignity of all human offices. Finally, he saw in Mary Magdalene, the innumerable and sacred multitude of converted sinners who found in repentance the nuptial robe saturated with the blood of the Lamb.

On seeing the little flock, *pusillus grex,* as He Himself called the ocean of the elect, the Savior remains silent about all of them, except for his Mother and for Saint John. He says to his Mother: *Woman, here is your son;* and to St. John: *Here is your mother.* These were the only words on the cross that were related to simple affections of the heart. All his other words came from eternal life and returned to it. Mary Magdalene was no more distinguished than the others; her triumph would not lie in feelings nor in the quality of her holiness. Jesus Christ waited for her on another stage, at a more pleasant moment. It was there, in placing the seal of her predestination, that, for her, He reserved graces that no one else had received before nor since.

The tomb opened up below the cross. The Son of man was laid down as one of us, guarded by two soldiers, as if death had not been sufficient to annihilate his power, and that a mysterious victory could have come out of His grave. This grave, in fact, remained if not as the object of hope at least as the meeting place of a piety that survived everything. Mary Magdalene was there; she was the first, as if in a place that was hers, and whose custody she earned by the prophetic tenderness of her two-fold anointing. In this encounter all the evangelists grant her the character of primacy. On the very evening of the passion, which indicates that she had not left Calvary, she saw the place where the body of the Lord was laid. It is St. Mark who clearly tells us. The Sabbath over, when the dawn of Sunday had not yet risen, she set out with the holy women, all of them carrying aromatics and perfumes. But the first rays of the sun showed them that the stone of the sepulcher had been set aside, and that the sepulcher was empty. While they were struck with dismay, without a thought of the mystery that was taking place, two angels appeared to them saying: *Why are you seeking among the dead one who is alive? He is no longer here, he has risen.* (Lk 24:5-7)

Troubled, bewildered, the holy women hastened to Jerusalem to report what they had seen and heard. The apostles listened to them as if their words were words of delirium, *deliramenta*. Nonetheless, St. Peter and St. John rushed out; Magdalene alone followed them. They arrived at the monument; they entered: it contained nothing. The winding sheet was on the stone, the shroud for the head, set apart. The two apostles did not know what to think, and left. No one on earth had yet understood what had happened, not St. Peter, not St. John, or Mary Magdalene. A veil covered the eyes of all of them. Where was Jesus? Magdalene alone remained, alone from the holy women, alone from the apostles, alone from everyone, with the empty and so beloved tomb. Oh moment of love in combat with death, and not yet knowing that death had been conquered! St. John was the only one to tell us what was happening. Listen to him.

"Now Mary was standing outside the sepulcher, crying. While she cried, she bent down to look into the sepulcher. She saw two angels, dressed in white, seated one at the head, the other at the feet, where the body had been placed. These told her: 'Woman, why are you crying?' She told them: 'Because they have taken my Lord away and I do not know where they placed him.' Having said that, she backed out and saw Jesus standing there. But she did not know it was Jesus. Jesus said to her: 'Woman, why are you crying? Whom are you looking for?' Thinking that he was the gardener, she told him: 'Sir, if you have taken him away, tell me where you laid him and I will take him.' Jesus said to her: 'Mary' Mary turning around and said to him: 'Master.' Jesus said to her: 'Do not touch me, for I have not yet ascended to my Father; but go find my brothers and tell them: I am going up to my Father and your Father, toward my God and your God.' "

Mary Magdalene then went to inform the disciples: 'I have seen the Lord, and this is what he told me.' (Jn 20:1-18) Thus, in that solemn moment of the resurrection of the Savior, a moment that decided everything, of the victory of God over the world, of life over death, it was not to his mother that Jesus first appeared; it was not to St. Peter, the foundation of the Church and the summit of theology; it was not to St. John, the beloved disciple; it was to Mary Magdalene, that is to say, the converted sinner, to the sin that became love by repentance. The Savior had previously said: *There is more joy in heaven for a sinner who converts himself than for ninety-nine just persons who have no need of conversion.* (Lk 15:7) But it was surely a sublime translation of the words that the privilege given to Mary Magdalene of being the first to see the Son of God risen from the tomb, conqueror of the devil, of sin, of the world, of death, and of being the first to gain in that glimpse the certitude and the consolation of the eternal salvation of men. What love must have merited the glory of this apparition, and what feelings must have received this reward for love!

There is here an abyss wherein the behavior of man cannot penetrate any deeper than his heart. I understand this only part way, I catch a glimpse of it, I adore it, and, if I can do no more, at least I always pause for a reflexion that moves me on these words of the Gospel: *He first appeared to Mary Magdalene.* (Mk 16:9) It is there, on the forehead of that illustrious and blessed woman, that shines a star which does not fade, and which will rejoice to the end of the centuries all those who study, within a soul enlightened by God, the mysteries of his relationship with us. *And so, He first appeared to Mary Magdalene.* If we cannot understand well all that took place in the heart of both, in the heart of God who was giving to His dearest friend on earth the beginnings of a recovered life, and in the heart of the creature that received from its God this unheard of mark of preference, at least we can follow the Gospel with the modesty of tender admiration, and seek in it, in the shadow of our failings, the imperfect joy that it available to us here below.

Up to now all the words we have heard regarding Mary Magdalene had not been addressed to her directly. When Jesus said about her: *Many sins will be forgiven her because she has loved much*, it was to Simon the Pharisee that He spoke in this way. When He said: *Mary has chosen the better part, that will not be taken from her*, it was to Martha that he answered. When He said: *Everywhere that this Gospel will be preached, in the whole world, what she has done will be told, for her glory*, it was to His disciples that He made this announcement. Here, for the first time, at the entrance to the tomb, on the morning of His resurrection, Jesus speaks directly to Mary, never to take up this conversation again save in the inaccessible region where His ascension will take Him. It is the crowning, the farewell, the page on which Magdalene will disappear from the Gospel and enter for the rest of her life into the dark avenues of history. Let us kiss with love these final words falling from the lips of Christ into the soul of His friend, and study them for the pleasure of our faith and the charm of our unfinished pilgrimage.

Woman, why are you crying? He had never said this to her on the day of her conversion, when she was weeping at his feet. Now the time for tears had passed; repentance, the cross, the tomb, all disappear in the triumphal splendors of the resurrection. Mary must cry only those tears that are eternal in the heart of saints because it is God who causes them and the ecstasy that spreads them.

Whom do you seek? There is nothing left to look for. Mary, you have found Him whom you will never lose again. You will no longer see Him on the cross in the bonds of death. You will no longer go to His tomb to embalm Him with the perfume of charity. You will no longer ask about Him to anyone on earth, to anyone in heaven, least of all to Him, because He is your soul, and your soul is Him. Separated for a time, you have gotten together in the location where there is no more space, no fence, no shade, nothing that will impede union and harmony. You are one as He wished and as you had hoped — one such as God is in his Son, in the depths of that essence that you inhabit by grace and that you will inhabit one day by glory.

Mary! Oh what feelings did this word convey! A feeling of reproach because Magdalene had not recognized Jesus; a feeling of revelation by the reproach. *Mary!* Alas! Yet, even here below how sweet is this name in the mouth of a friend, and how deeply does it penetrate into the painful depths of our being! And if it were God who pronounced it softly, if it were God who died for us, who rose for us, who called us by our name — what echo would it not produce in the infinite depths of our misery! Mary Magdalene heard everything as contained in her name: she heard the mystery of the resurrection, which she did not understand; she heard there the love of her Savior, and in that love she recognized him. *Master!* She replied. One word was enough for her, just as one word was all it took for the Son of God. The more souls love each other, the more their speech is short.

Do not touch me for I have not yet ascended to my Father. Twice Jesus Christ had allowed Magdalene to touch him, and twice he praised her for it. And now, after His resurrection, when His body has already been transfigured by a superior life, He opposes the chaste eagerness of Mary. He does not wish her to approach Him with those hands that previously had perfumed His feet and His head. Why this unexpected strictness? And how could the resurrection hold back the former familiarity of a tested tenderness? It is because Jesus is no longer who He was, the object for everyone of a contact that encourages faith, and of a charity that is caught up in the conversations of life. He is between earth and heaven, still visible for several days, but on His way to the Father and it is only there, where all flesh will be transformed like His own, that He wishes to be touched and possessed by His own. He gives to Mary Magdalene in this harsh lesson, an indication that one must aim higher, that from now on Bethany is in the bosom of the Father who had sent His Son and where the Son will rejoin Him to prepare for His friends the place of embrace that will have no end. Do not touch the Son of man because He has not yet ascended to His Father, and you yourself, Mary, you have not yet ascended there. Your lips, pure as they are, stamped with the fire that the seraphim of repentance and that of love have left, are not able to give to the glorious body of Christ the marks of tenderness purified by death. We have to die with Jesus to touch Jesus again. Only then will you and He be like each other; only then, will you carry to His feet the perfume of resurrection and deposit there the virginal breath of immortality reconquered.

Go find my brothers and tell them: I am going up to my Father and your Father, to my God and your God. These were the last words of the Savior to Mary Magdalene They give her, in preference to all others, the revelation of the mystery that will close the passage of the Son of God among us in the work of our redemption. Apostle of the ascension for the apostles themselves, Magdalene preserved that trait all the rest of her life. We will see her gravitate toward Christ, who disappeared in the clouds, by a greatness of soul that will not surprise us at all because we believe in the marvels of the charity that aims upward just as we believe in the marvels of the charity that extends downward.

CHAPTER VI

Mary Magdalene in Provence

Jesus is no longer in this world by a visible presence. He left behind his apostles, his mother, His friends of the heart, but leaving to each one a life and a death that He predestined. St. Peter died in Rome with the torment of his Master; all the apostles confirmed their faith by martyrdom. St. John himself was not fully spared; at Rome, before the Latin gate, he suffered severe punishment but he escaped death only by preserving the glory of the immolation to which he consented. Nonetheless, it is clear that the Savior watched over him in the memory of the preference that He had granted him. Escaping from the trial by a miracle, from exile by the death of a hated tyrant, he passed his days in an old age that caught the attention of the entire Church, and that allowed him to give to the divinity of Jesus Christ, in the final and most sublime of the Gospels, an undeniable testimony. It fell to him also, by a unique privilege in the New Testament, to see prophetically the future of the Church. He dictated this revelation in a format that one day will enlighten and strengthen in their tribulations the elect of the final days of time. He died after that, filled with peace, and knowing only to repeat to Christians those words fallen from the mouth of Jesus Christ into his own: "My children, love one another." The Mother of Jesus did not survive very long days between the resurrection and the ascension of her beloved Son. She felt carried to him by a desire that untied in the depth of her soul all that held her captive, and from her tomb, immediately visited by life, she rose to the throne where she reigns forever over the angels and the men saved by the fruit of her womb.

Just as the Mother of God and St. John, Mary Magdalene will not end her days by martyrdom. She will live in the tranquil blessing of His love. She will live at the feet of the disappeared Jesus Christ, just as she lived at Bethany and at Calvary, a lover used to the delights of contemplation, and having as her only need to gaze on the soul of Him whom she formerly saw under the transparent veil of human flesh. But what kind of hidden or celebrated haven would have been prepared for her? Where would she hide the blessed remains of her existence? Would it be the deserts of the East, the shores of the Jordan, the mountains of Zion, the thatched hut of Nazareth or of Bethlehem? Who will be the last witnesses of her unapproachable charity? Jesus Christ had left his Mother to Jerusalem, St. Peter to Rome, St. John to Asia; to whom would he bequeath Mary Magdalene?

We already know: it was France that received from the hand of God that part of the testament of His Son. Tradition, history, the monuments vied with each other to tell us, and Providence took care to give their testimony invincible clarity. One cannot set his foot on the soil of Provence without striking the memory of St. Mary Magdalene. Present everywhere, she does not live there in the shape of a solitary accident; she is linked to the reality that holds first place in the history of all Christian people, and of the important matter of their conversion. And nothing, no doubt, perpetuated itself more stubbornly in the memory of a race or of a country than this change wrought in beliefs and practices by a new worship, proscribed and triumphant because of the influence of its virtues. In like manner, is there any Christian nation that has not kept the memory of its early apostles, that has honored their tomb, built churches in their name, invoked their help, and laughs at the useless arguments of a blind knowledge against this popular and very powerful tradition? Provence was not an uncultured tribe when Christianity appeared; for more than a century it had been a Roman province. It had received from its masters all the culture of Rome and from this source, all that of Greece. It was bound by Marseille to all the banks of the Mediterranean; untiring ships brought it the tribute of faraway shores. Then, when the first sound of the Gospel reached its ears, it could not be mistaken about those who brought to it from the East this noble revelation. She knew them, judged them, and once converted by them to this new law, their names were sacred like no other name had been up to that time. Who can doubt this? Who cannot see that a nation, especially when it is a question of religion, has a memory more certain than that of man, and that age, instead of altering it, renews it unceasingly? What is engraved on the altar by worship and lies in the heart by prayer, lasts longer than marble and bronze; kings who have only history to live on assuredly have less than what is given to their leaders by the soul of generations.

Now, from whom does Provence date its faith? Whom does it thank, after nineteen centuries, for having received, the day after the Gospel, a ray of light that had just appeared over the deep darkness of the human race? It is thanks to that illustrious family of Bethany who had Jesus Christ as guest and friend, to Lazarus, to Martha, to Mary Magdalene along with their companions Trophimus and Maximinus. These are the names that sons learned from their fathers, and that the fathers had received from the gratitude of their ancestors. Marseille wished to have St. Lazarus as its first bishop; Aix attributed its glory to St. Maximinus; Arles to St. Trophimus; Avignon and Tarascon named Martha as the apostle who delivered them from error; and St. Mary Magdalene, united to all these people by a memory that rests on their own while surpassing it, floats over the entire Church of Provence like the sovereign of the apostolate that founded her.

The memorials agree with this acclamation of the centuries. It was in vain that the barbarians covered Provence with their hordes; it was in vain that, renewing their furor after it was pacified, the

Saracens added to the ruins already made their protracted and terrible blows of scimitar. These ruins, twice brought about, were unable to prevail against the memorials that the people and Providence had intended to perpetuate the memory of the holy founders of the Church in Provence. Marseille can still see in the cellars of the ancient Abbey of St. Victor the crypt where, under Lazarus, the first Christians that it produced for God, and where the body itself of the its first bishop rested until the day when it was withdrawn from the ravages of Islam by a transfer that benefitted the church of Autun. Tarascon venerated the tomb that held the relics of St. Martha, where it still preserves them, and whose marble, stronger than time, and despite its mutilation, allows the pilgrim to recognize the lively scene of the resurrection of Lazarus. Two other tombs, even more famous, two tombs united in the same crypt by a fraternal piety, recall to the voyager that St. Magdalene lay there, facing St. Maximinus, and that the very name of St. Maximinus, given to the place where this double and unique burial took place, attests to the impression that it produced on the people, one that was never extinguished. It was there that St. Magdalene ended her pilgrimage; it was here that St. Maximinus buried her in an alabaster sepulcher, in memory of that other alabaster in which twice the saint had enclosed the perfume with which she anointed the Savior. It was there that St. Maximinus himself wished to have his mortal remains placed, beside these other remains so dear to his heart, to Jesus Christ, to the angels, to men, and where there comes to find her a veneration soon to be twenty centuries old.

The tomb of St. Maximinus represents the apostolic mission given to him by Jesus Christ. That of St. Magdalene retains the traces of various traits in the life of the Son of God. On the frieze that the piety of the faithful has more than mutilated, could be seen formerly, from ancient and irrefutable testimonies, her anointing of her well-beloved Master.

All these tombs, linked together by the divine relationship of time, of persons, and of holiness, bear the mark of the early ages of Christianity. First of all, the Roman style is recognized with the unusual mixture, familiar at the time, of Christian subjects with symbols of idolatry. There is no archeologist who has not been struck by them; the avowals of the less credulous confirmed the respect attached to those ancient and faithful witnesses.

And they were not the only ones. The liturgy of a number of churches agrees with them and with tradition; finally, history itself, in support of tradition, the memorials and the liturgy, affixed the seal of a demonstration behind all this splendor. For a long time, it was believed that no pen of an ancient writer had touched on the life of St. Magdalene and engraved her records on the solidity of history. The primitive and continuous silence of human writings stood in opposition to the beliefs of peoples, to the mute language of marble, to the feasts and readings of the Church, to the connection of all the proofs. The question was asked: where was the history of St. Magdalene if, before the eleventh or the twelfth century, in the libraries of Europe, were found only traces of a biography dedicated to a woman who had so naturally seduced the heart and inspired the genius of saints? But Providence was watching. At Oxford, in one of the twenty-four colleges of that famous university — a college still dedicated today to St. Mary Magdalene — some pious hands discovered a manuscript carrying the name of Rabanus Maurus, archbishop of Mayence at the beginning of the ninth century, and containing the lives of St. Martha and of St. Mary Magdalene. The authenticity of this manuscript was verified by the grouping of the characters who placed their belief in the archeology of the date of the work, of its reliability, and of its integrity.

We will not enter into details, which are given elsewhere. We will limit ourselves to say that in the ninth century, Rabanus Maurus, by his knowledge, his piety, his influence, his fame, and his honors, was one of the most illustrious men of his times. Abbot of Fulda for twenty years, voluntarily retired by resignation to a deep solitude, then called in spite of himself to the see of Mayence, he shone in his century by everything that could be praised by posterity, by the accuracy

64

and the sincerity of a historian. His biography of St. Martha and of St. Mary Magdalene was well-balanced. He followed the Gospel step by step and when the Gospel faded away in the ascension of Our Lord, he interested himself in writings that he declared were very ancient and were the foundation of his account.

Now these ancient writings were found, just as his were; they were found in the public libraries of Paris — pages all the more precious and venerable since in comparing them to the history of Rabanus Maurus, we recognize them therein, almost word for word. In the testimony of the archbishop of Mayence, they are like so many others before the ninth century, since he called them ancient. In fact, in their natural tone and their brevity, the reveal the taste of a century that had not yet known, regarding saints, the hollow exaggeration of a deceitful bombast. It is estimated that these writings date from the fifth or sixth century, namely, at a time when all the records of the apostolate of St. Magdalene and of her companions in Provence were still young, where the invasion of the barbarians and that of the Saracens had destroyed nothing of the claims of our churches, and where, consequently, it was easy to draw from them genuine and certain records in order to write them down.

Thus it was that time, instead of weakening the glory of St. Mary Magdalene, had prepared her resurrection. What passes today as the Bible of

Christianity, whose veracity is confirmed by the very passage of ages, has also passed for the Bible of St. Magdalene. Deeper knowledge clothed tradition with a brighter light; taking up henceforth the life of our very dear and illustrious saint at the empty tomb of the Savior, we can follow its course on the fortunate land of Provence.

CHAPTER VII

From St. Mary Magdalene

to Sainte-Baume and to St. Maximinus

The persecution of Christianity had begun in Jesus Christ. It did not delay in spreading around His tomb. St. Stephen, after his Master, was the second martyr; soon, St. Paul carried Christianity to Damascus while he himself waited to become an illustrious victim. Blood calls for blood; one does not stop on this road until he is choked by a flood that keeps rising and finally reaches the lips of those who produced it. Christianity experienced its baptism at the same waters as its founder; its first disciples, dispersed by the cross where they were born, carried far the word that was to enlighten the world, and the blood that was to purify it. It was the second emigration of the human race. The first had brought about nations, the second would make the Church. Anyone who saw these men leaving Jerusalem by all its gates and taking the road of all winds, would no doubt have taken them as common travelers. At the time, only God knew the secret of His breath and the difference there was between this departure and that of Babel.

One ship, among others, left these lovely shores that stretch from Carmel to the mouths of the Nile. It carried in its narrow interior the family of Bethany and some disciples who had joined themselves to its blessing. The same hand that lead all the apostles also led them. Under its invisible impetus, hidden by that of the waves, it reached a city that even then was one of the gateways to Europe. Marseille saw them enter without knowing the treasure that came with them. Whoever would have named Lazarus, Mary Magdalene, Martha, would have said nothing to its ear, even less to its heart. Glory had not yet been born for Christianity; it came as an unknown and those who were to erect scaffolds, to prepare some temples for it, did not yet know its name or its works. Its power lay hidden behind humility, and the earth passed beside heaven without realizing it.

Solitary places, underground crypts came to celebrate in the shadows the august mysteries of redemption. A small flock was formed from the blood brought from the cross by those who had seen it flow. Sailors, perhaps, workers, poor women composed this Church, originating around the risen one of Bethany. Time ripened this crop and increased it. Marseille was finally moved by the news of this new doctrine; the blood of Lazarus gave it its first martyr as well as its first page in the book of life that it keeps writing every day.

What Mary Magdalene's role was in the apostolate of her brother, we do not know. There remains in Marseille only a memory of her, such as an altar that bears her name in the burial vaults of the Abbey of St. Victor, a venerable and meaningful memory, since these vaults are the oldest monuments of the Christian faith in Marseille, and are like its catacombs.

It was at Aix that the traces of St. Magdalene began to grow. In the first years of this century, one could still see an oratory venerated for having been the place where she prayed with St. Maximinus, the privileged companion of her pilgrimage. It carried the name of Holy Savior, and was placed in a side nave of the cathedral, even though it broke the architectural lines, so strong was the tradition that regarded it as the cradle of Christianity in the capital of Provence. But Aix, no more than Marseille, was to be the predestined location where Jesus Christ awaited his ancient and faithful friend to have her enjoy that *part that she had preferred and that no one was to take from her, as He had solemnly promised*. That part was contemplation in solitude.

Solitude did exist. God, who created everything in view of the future, and who did not sketch a shoreline, raise up a mountain, water a valley, or dig a sea without knowing for what people or what souls He was working; God, in creation, had thought of Mary Magdalene and had made for her, at a certain point of the earth, a particular haven. I described it in the first pages of this book [i.e., In Praise of Provence]. I named it before anything else *Sainte-Baume*, as the center where it called Christian hearts to rest from the world and to venerate the sublime mystery of the love of God. One benefit attracted Mary Magdalene, the same grace that had chosen her, though a sinner, led her to the foot of the cross, and made her, at the gates of death, the first spectator of the resurrection of the Son of God. She came as she had gone to Jesus Christ by the same light and the same impulse. This is how the extensive retreats of the Thebaid [in Egypt] were peopled. Thus did St. Anthony discover, between the Nile and the Red Sea, the mountain of Kolsin, where he ruled over the deserts and generations of hermits; thus, from century to century, saints touched with their feet unknown grounds, blessed them, fertilized them with their divine sweat, and sowed that glory which survived everything because it is not a daughter of time. Mary Magdalene belonged to that race of all those founders , and closer than they to the trunk from which they all sprang, she had brought to the sacred height of *Sainte-Baume* virtue that had no equal, to leave a memory that had no tomb.

The Holy Places are for the world what stars are for the sky: a source of light, of heat, and of life. When we ask why God consecrated this mountain or that valley, we could as well ask why He threw down from heaven an immobile star that guided our sons and our brothers on the waves of the ocean. Ah! Would that it had pleased God to make less rare those places where love had lived!

Would to God that our heart had found more often on this cold earth some embers to warm us! But this is the case with the holy as with the great; if grace is as thrifty as nature, at least we ought to recognize its works and not reject its miracles.

St. Paul used to say: I know a man in Christ, not fourteen years ago, whether in his body, I do not know, or out of his body, I do not know, God knows, who was raised to the third heaven; and I know a man, whether in his body or out of it, I do not know, God knows, who was raised up to paradise and who heard secret words that man is not permitted to utter. (II Cor 12:2-4)

What Saint Paul was unable to say no one else will say; but his very powerlessness reveals a lot to us. It gives us the strength to follow Mary Magdalene in her solitude and to assist without surprise at the marvels of her contemplation. There, apart from the men who had crucified the Savior of the world, she kept only one thought: that of recovering the divine friend she had lost. Indeed, neither distance nor death break apart genuine love; it digs all the deeper into the soul as it is deprived of overflowing outside. If we have seen lives fade on the tomb of a son or of a spouse, what would it have been for Mary Magdalene who had held the feet of the Son of God and who had loved him beyond all friendship of nature and all anointing of grace? Moreover, I am not surprised when tradition tells me that every day, and seven times a day, she was removed from her grotto at the summit of the rock that covers it, to hear in that place what Saint Paul declared having heard without being able to express it.

Oh holy raptures! Man, a stranger to God and to His Christ does not understand you. Bound to the earth by the weight of sin, he does not know what kind of control God has over a holy soul, and what power that holy soul has on its body. He believes in the attractions of worlds, but not in the attraction of God. Let him keep the knowledge that flatters his pride, but for us, simple children of the Gospel, who have seen our God die out of love and return to heaven by the same love, we should know that this is our route, our hope, our eternal future. We thank God who has given us in his saints, even here below, examples of the ecstasy where his vision will plunge us.

The *Sainte-Baume* was the Thabor of St. Mary Magdalene. More blessed than St. Peter who said to the Lord on the day of his transfiguration: *It is good for us to be here; let us set up three tents*. Magdalene saw this tent refused to the prince of the apostles. She lived as a recluse, between the penances of the grotto and the rapture of the height. There, nothing changed, no more than at Thabor. Faith, the respectful worshiper of all lofty memories, again resides on the two mountains, and from their immaculate summits, she gazes on high the God who visits them.

For thirty years, God provided this spectacle to his angels to leave a remembrance of it for all centuries. For thirty years, Mary Magdalene went from repentance to glory, and from glory to repentance, uniting in this alternative the double life that she had lived, that of a sinful woman and that of friend of Jesus. In the interior of her grotto, behind a venerated grill, there rises a rock where tradition reports that she prayed, and which, alone, in that humid location, maintained a pious and perpetual dryness. Outside, on the steep ledge and the highest of the mountain, is the point marked by tradition as that where Magdalene was raised every day. A chapel, called the *Holy Pillar*, consecrates its ground and attracts the veneration of pilgrims.

Yet the hour came when St. Magdalene was to pass form her earthly and interrupted ecstasy to the everlasting ecstasy of eternity. She knew that, and for a last time before dying, she wished to receive in the form of Eucharistic bread the body and blood of her Savior. When someone supports himself on the wall of the terrace that lies in front of *Sainte-Baume*, he has at his back the mountain itself, which runs from west to east in a parallel line with the Mediterranean Sea. Facing him is another chain, lower and less forbidding, that seems to come from Marseille and close to the *Sainte-Baume*, ends abruptly in a sheer slope; this is Mount Aurelian. Beyond it, like a rear guard of the horizon, lies the savage and demanding brow of *Sainte-Victoire*, that famous mountain at whose feet Marius defied the Cimbers and the Teutons [barbarian tribes]. This triple rampart leaves no passage for the eye, except toward the east. There, a vast and deep plain spreads out, ended by the Alps, but which, close to the viewer, has as its courtyard another narrow and circular plain formed by the hills that descend together from Mount Aurelian, the *Sainte-Baume*, and the *Sainte-Victoire*. It is the plain of St. Maximinus, placed in sharp contrast between two historic events the most unlike in the world, between the name of Mary Magdalene and that or Marius [a Roman general]. St. Maximinus had an oratory built there under a similar impulse that had led Mary Magdalene to the *Sainte-Baume*. Both of them, one on the mountain, the other in the plain, could see the haven where God had set them close without distracting them.

Then, when the inhabitant above felt the hour of her recall, she was, according to tradition, carried by angels to the side of the Aurelian Way, at a point where this road cuts the route that still leads from the *Sainte-Baume* to St. Maximinus. A famous pillar, called the *Holy Pillar*, recalls to the traveler this memorable event of the saint's passage. From the top, we can see her supported by angels who seem to move her from one place to another. A few steps away, rose the modest oratory of St. Maximinus, near the town called *Tegulata* on the itinerary of Antoninus. There, the bishop was awaiting the friend of his Master. He received her, gave her Communion of the body and blood of Christ; then, grasped by the repose of death, she fell asleep peacefully. St. Maximinus laid her body in a tomb of alabaster, he himself preparing the sepulcher, facing the monument where he had buried the relics that were to bring immortal renown to this forgotten corner of the world.

This was the belief of peoples and the belief of the Church, as were tradition, history, the communication of places and times. Never did so much glory give more authority to the miracles of God within a soul. In fact, we will see the effects on this tomb of a series of events, which, by themselves, would be a demonstration that underneath that stone, there lay an admirable object of divine Providence and of the preference of God.

Every holy place needs a watchman to preserve it from profanation and from being overlooked. This is a law of the supernatural world. But in the early days of the Church, when persecution raged against her on all sides, it was of considerable benefit for Her to have crypts, catacombs, and tombs. There, under the earth, she hid the blood of her martyrs; only a humble piety kept watch over this mysterious deposit. Some paintings, poorly rendered, a few words badly written, kept alive in those deserted regions the vigilant memory of the faithful. While the Caesars surrounded their crimes with brilliant immortality, Christians, buried under their palaces, raised to unknown virtues the humble bronze of a peaceful memory. Then came the century when all the shadows of Christ were dispelled. Emerging victorious from this other sepulcher, He appeared with his saints to a world astonished to see Him. Crypts opened themselves, catacombs lit up, tombs became temples, and a guard more secure than the one that watched at the threshold of the Capitol or the Palatine Palace, grouped themselves around these new glories to confirm their origin and to perpetuate their antiquity. Such was the case of the prominent bluff of the *Sainte--Baume* and of the tomb of St. Magdalene. As early as the fourth century, a wind from the east had brought to the Gauls the renown and the examples of the hermits of the Thebaide: St. Martin of Tours, St. Honoratus at the islands of Lerins, the priest Cassian at Marseille, had been the first promoters of the cenobitic life among us. Cassian, the last arrival of these three, had visited the monasteries of Egypt, and recalled to mind in famous writings their institutions and their practices. On his return to Marseille, his homeland, he had founded the Abbey of St. Victor, on the very crypts where St. Lazarus had his tomb. But as a lover of solitude, in which he had seen so many majestic spectacles, he did not delay in looking for a haven where he could sometimes escape the noise of the crowds and of men. The *Sainte-Baume* naturally touched his heart, and nothing, no doubt, could remind him more of his admiration of the Nile. And so, he came with a few of his followers, and placed that guard which, for a thousand years between the 4th and the 13th centuries, remained faithful to the memory of the relics that Providence had entrusted to him. Established at the same time at the *Sainte-Baume* and at St. Maximinus, at the place of the rapture and the place of burial, the Cassianite religious showed themselves worthy of the choice that had been made of them for this two-fold monument of divine grace.

Still today, we can see, just below the *Sainte-Baume*, near the east, a hermitage called the hermitage of Cassian. Very near it, there is a fountain of fresh water called the fountain of Cassian. The mountain that dominates this primitive wilderness carries the same name. The shepherds who wandered with their flocks on the nearby steep areas had no other way of labeling the mountain, the hermitage, and the fountain. They do not know who Cassian was, but they repeat his name to travelers; the faithful echo of tradition repeats it after them, without knowing any more than they do.

At the beginning of the 17th century, the Saracens poured into Provence and sowed now and then a devastation that lasted three hundred years. The Cassianites, trembling for the relics of St. Magdalene, made the crypt that contained them disappear under a mass of sand and of earth. Thus, without realizing it, they prepared a future and magnificent disclosure of the saint. Not satisfied with having hidden to eyes and mounded

up the tomb, they pushed their caution to the point
of disturbing the interior order. The body of St.
Magdalene had been placed at the bottom of the
crypt, on the left, in an alabaster tomb, that of St.
Maximinus, on the right, facing the other. In time,
a third and a fourth tomb were added to the
primitive monuments. Sidoine, bishop of Aix, had
wanted to be buried in the crypt, next to the
founder of his Church; accordingly, he had been
buried on the right of the entrance. Opposite him,
and therefore on the left, on the side of St.
Magdalene, another marble received some relics
that were called the *Holy Innocents*, either
because they were brought from Palestine, or were
simply the bodies of children who died in early
age, before the grace of baptism. Now the
Cassianites, the better to disguise from research
the very previous deposit that had been entrusted
to them, transported them from the famous
alabaster where they reposed, into the tomb of
Saint Sidoine previously emptied of the remains
of that bishop; there, they placed two inscriptions
that would one day testify to the truth of the body
of St. Magdalene.

That day was now near. Almost six centuries
would pass by after these acts of fearful piety. The
ravages of the Saracens extended way beyond all
that had been foreseen. When, finally, these
ended, the memory of the place where lay
precisely the remains of the saint was also
dissolved. It was known that they lay below the
floor of the basilica, and were venerated there. But

no authority, no hand was raised to bring her out
of the shadows accumulated over her by time.
God allowed this so as to make her disclosure
more startling, as well as to allow in the meantime
for the veneration of the friend of his Son a
brilliance that would fill France, Europe, and
Asia.

It was the period of the Crusades. Little by
little, a contemporary rumor had spread
concerning their origin around the Abbey of
Vezelay in Burgundy. This abbey, founded in the
9th century by Gérard de Roussillon, count and
governor of Provence, had long existed without
any renown. Towards the end of the 11th century,
whether there was good faith, or whether there
was skill, one got to hear and to repeat that the
body of St. Magdalene, removed from St.
Maximinus by Gérard de Roussillon, lay at the
ancient abbey, under the main altar. This rumor
having gained firmness, the bishop of Autun, on
whom the abbey did not depend because it was
under the immediate jurisdiction of the Holy See,
but who was the diocesan bishop, thought it was
his duty to prevent the pilgrimage that was
beginning and was forming under a belief that he
did not share. He made an appeal to the Holy See.
The Sovereign Pontiff, Pascal II, rescinded the
ordinance of the bishop by a bull dated in 1203,
authorized the pilgrimage, and invited to it all
classes of French people. It was a movement hard
to imagine. You could say that all of France
flocked to Vezelay; this place became so

important in public and pious opinion that Louis VII went there with St. Bernard in 1147 to preach the second crusade. A multitude of lords and knights took the cross under the impression made on them by the saintly abbot of Clairvaux. From then on, the veneration of St. Magdalene was closely linked to the enthusiasm of the crusades. Penitents devoted to the deliverance of the Holy Sepulcher as reparation for their faults, the crusaders naturally found in Mary Magdalene, the converted sinner, a protection for their arms. They could not carry to that profaned sepulcher a more worthy name and memory of it than those of the woman who had so loved Jesus Christ, who, at the very entrance to His tomb, had deserved to be the first to see Him, glorified by the resurrection. In this way Europe gave back to Asia the treasure it had received from it. Mary Magdalene returned to Bethany under the banner of Christianity. Her name, blended with the acclamations of victory or of the martyrdom of defeat, reminded the knights of all the mysteries of which she was a witness. They themselves found in their battlefields, a sorrowful road and a triumphant one.

In 1190, Philippe Augustus and Richard the Lion-Hearted arranged to meet at Vezelay to prepare the third expedition to the Holy Land. Similar feelings produced similar effects. Finally, later on, when St. Louis was on the eve of heading for the second time towards the East, in 1267, he came to Vezelay to close the era of the crusades and to tender to Mary Magdalene an homage that was the last she was to receive in a place that had not been her own. Indeed, in spite of the crowd of pilgrims and the renown of the spectacles that had taken place there, time had not confirmed the error that was its basis. The protests of the bishop of Autun were always remembered, but the question remained: on what grounds was the belief based that the body of St. Magdalene was moved from St. Maximinus to Vezelay. A remarkable indication was found of this disposition of minds in the trip that St. Louis, on return from the first crusade, in 1254, made to St. Maximinus and the *Sainte-Baume,* and which is also reported in his biography by Sir de Joinville: "After these things, the king left for Yères and came to the city of Aix in Provence, to honor the blessed Magdalene, who lay at about a day's journey away, and we reached a place called *La Baume*, in a high crag, where it was said that the holy Magdalene had lived as a hermit for a long time." It was impossible for Sir de Joinville not to know the claims of the Abbey of Vezelay, and yet he stated unhesitatingly that the body of St. Magdalenee lay *a short day's journey* away near Aix.

The secret of God could no longer remain hidden. The error of Vezelay had exalted St. Magdalene and bound her memory with that of the greatest military and religious movement ever seen in the world. It has also given solemn dedication to the certitude of her coming to Provence and of her burial at St. Maximinus.

There remained to forge at St. Maximinus the same chain of that glory, so as finally to present to the piety of the world and to its gaze the undisputed relics of the illustrious penitent. This required pure hands, a heart known to God and to men, a sovereign authority, striking evidence of truth. We shall see that, in fact, Providence had thought of that long before.

St. Louis had a nephew, born of his brother Charles of Anjou, king of Sicily and count of Provence. This nephew was also called Charles, and after the death of his father he became king of Sicily and count of Provence under the name Charles II. He had a great fondness for St. Magdalene that he got from his family. Although this was common to all French chivalry, in him it had a higher degree of enthusiasm and of sincerity. Since he was at the time only prince of Salerno, God inspired him with the thought of penetrating into the mystery that for six centuries cloaked the tomb of the one woman he loved for his love of Jesus Christ. He went to St. Maximinus, without ostentation, with some gentlemen in his company. After having questioned the religious and some old persons, he had a trench opened in the old basilica of Cassian. On 9 December 1279, after unfruitful efforts up to that point, he himself after having removed his military cloak, took a mattock and dug the earth with his workers. Shortly, the stone of a tomb was struck. It was that of St. Sidoine, at the right of the crypt. The prince ordered the removal of the

82

entablature; immediately, a perfume arose, telling him that the grace of God was close. He bent down an instant, had the sepulcher closed up, placed his official seal and called together the bishops of Provence to have them assist in the recognition of the relics.

Nine days later, on 18 December, in the presence of the archbishops of Arles and of Aix, of many other prelates and gentlemen, the prince had the seal he had placed on the sarcophagus broken. The sarcophagus was opened and the hand of the prince, on scattering the dust that covered the bones, came upon an object that broke with age in his fingers. It was a piece of cork from which a sheet of parchment fell, with its writing still legible. It contained what follows: *The year of the birth of the Savior 710, the sixth day of the month of December, under the reign of Eudes, very pious king of the French, at the time of the ravages by the treacherous nation of Saracens, the body of the very cherished and venerable Mary Magdalene was very secretly and during the night transferred from her alabaster sepulcher into this one, which is made of marble, and from which the body of Sidoine was removed the better to hide it and shelter it from the said treacherous nation.*

The king Eudes mentioned in the inscription was Eudes of Aquitaine, who declared himself independent when Pepin the Short seized the kingdom of Austrasia, and who governed France supremely in the south of the Loire.

The act of inscription and the manner in which it was discovered was drawn up by the prince, the archbishops and the bishops present. At the height of his joy, Charles, after having again sealed the tomb, convoked for 5 May of the following year an assembly of prelates, counts, barons, knights, judges, from Provence as from surrounding areas, to assist in the solemn transfer of the relics he had, in a way, just brought back to life, or at least withdrawn from the darkness of a long series of centuries. Fame spread its miraculous circumstances. On 12 May 1280, a considerable multitude of notables and of common folk were standing at the tomb of St. Mary Magdalene. This was the first time that the tribute around her body took on royal proportions. Buried in alabaster, in a modest crypt, it had passed through the age of persecution to that of barbarity, always venerated, always loved, but without any fanfare attending this veneration and this love. The very steps taken to save it ended up by digging into the memory of men an even deeper tomb than the one where it rested. Now, gold and precious stones would succeed the alabaster, a basilica of first order to the humble oratory of St. Maximinus, a celebrated monastery to the small cloister of the Cassianites. Kings and pontiffs would come to this tomb in such great numbers that the steps of bishops and of lofty lords will no longer be counted, and after the tomb of Our Lord and of his apostle St. Peter there will

be in the world no tomb comparable to that of
Mary Magdalene.

On a third time, then, in the presence of an
illustrious and countless gathering, the prince of
Salerno had the tomb he had sealed opened; the
seals were found to be intact. The head of the
saint was whole, except for the lower jaw, which
was missing. The tongue was there, dried out but
stuck to the palate. To the eye, the limbs were but
bones laid bare of flesh, but a delightful perfume
enveloped these remains brought to the light of
day and to the piety of souls. They were removed
from their layer of dust, to be venerated more
closely. All eyes were on that forehead which had
laid on the feet of Our Savior, on those empty
cavities that had been filled with the loveliest
tears that ever flowed before God, on that tongue
that had spoken of Jesus Christ to Jesus Christ, on
the bones that had bowed before Him and had
adored Him, on this entire dead being that faith
brought to life and whose actions were revived at
the same time. An everlasting glory had been
promised to Mary Magdalene by an infallible
mouth; this glory, everyone could see, could feel
it, could breath it into themselves and feel it in
others. Thirteen centuries had passed over this
body and it was still there; without voice, or life,
or soul, and yet immortal. After having looked,
one looked again and the impressiveness of
Christianity completed the scene by moving the
actors and the witnesses to a marvelous flight
towards God. It was already known that a special

sign, altogether divine, has been recognized on the forehead of Magdalene. It was a flap of skin, mobile and transparent that glowed at the left temple, on the right, consequently, of the viewer; this inspired everyone at the same moment, by a unanimous act of faith, that it was there, right there, at that blessed spot, that the Savior had touched Magdalene when He told her after the resurrection: *Noli me tangere. — Do not touch Me.* There was no proof of this. But what could one believe on seeing in the spot so palpable a trace of life, one that had stubbornly resisted thirteen centuries of burial? Chance has no meaning for the Christian; there, where nature is evidently blessed in its laws, it rises immediately to the final cause, that cause which never acts without a reason, and whose reason it reveals to hearts that do not reject its enlightenment. Language has preserved the impression of those who were the first to see this bit of life remaining in the body of Mary Magdalene. Even today, it is called the *Noli me tangere*: a lofty name because it was created by faith for a thought worthy of her. Five centuries after the first transfer, the *Noli me tangere* still remained at the same place, with the same characteristics. A deputation from the court of the counts of Aix — composed of the first President, a Solicitor-General and two counselors — authenticated the discovery. It did not detach itself until 1780, on the eve of a time that would spare no memory and no relic. Even at that very moment, medical doctors called to testify by the highest court of the country, declared that the *Noli me tangere* had adhered to the forehead by the very force of a life that was preserved there. Charles divided the body in three parts: the head, which represented par excellence the heart of the saint; a bone from the right arm with which she had spread the perfume on the feet of Our Lord; finally, the other limbs that did not answer to any particular thought. By his care, the first of the relics was enclosed in a bust of gold, the face covered by a mask of crystal, the latter by a movable mask of gold. The father of the prince, Charles the 1ˢᵗ of Anjou, sent from Naples his own crown, made of gold and encrusted with gems, to have it repose forever on the head of the saint. The second relic, the bone of the right arm, was placed in a reliquary of gold-plated silver, itself in the form of an arm, and carried on a pedestal supported by four lions. The other members were transferred and sealed in a silver shrine. An inventive piety had thus measured the honor without dividing the glory.

One should not forget that in the course of transfer, when the bones were taken one by one, a second inscription was discovered, engraved on a wooden tablet, enveloped in a globe of wax. It bore these simple words: *Here lies the body of St. Mary Magdalene.*

The first step had been taken in the royal glorification of this most holy body. It had come out of the earth, victorious over the centuries, with a certitude that defied all unbelief, and pageantry that announced the progress of faith and of love in the hearts of men. A prince from the blood of St. Louis had dug the earth with his own hands to discover it; bishops had touched it with apprehension; a king had sent it his crown; gold, silver, and precious stones, artfully fashioned, from then on served as its bed and its ornament; innumerable people had greeted its discovery; and from one end to the other of Christianity, the report had moved all the friends who had loved her. But Rome, as the source of glory as it is of truth, had to sanction this solemn triumph by its approbation. Charles thought of this when the misfortunes of his family and relatives placed obstacles to his pious desires. Prisoner of Spain for six years, recalled to the throne after the death of his father, still a captive, for a long time he had waited for better days. Once freed, he went to Rome. It was Boniface VIII, a friend of the family, who occupied the Apostolic See. Charles presented him with the two handwritten inscriptions found in the tomb of St. Magdalene and attached to a document attesting to their authenticity by the signatures of a great number of prelates. He also opened before him the golden bust, enclosing the head of the saint; the Pope could see with his own eyes the extraordinary sign of life that death had preserved. As we said, the lower jaw was missing to the relic. Boniface noticed this, and remembering that at the church of St. John Lateran, there was kept a bone of this kind, he ordered that it be brought. The two relics closely placed together fit so perfectly that they left no doubt that they belonged to the same person, the same head.

Moved by what he had seen, Boniface VIII published, on the date of April 1295, a bull in which he recognized as genuine the finding of the body of St. Magdalene and authorized Charles II, king of Sicily and count of Provence — who deserved the merit for its discovery — to transfer the monastery of St. Maximinus of the Cassianite Order to that of the Friars Preachers. The latter, a new order in the Church, shone brightly and Charles thought it able to answer the purpose he had conceived to build at St. Maximinus, on the very place of the ancient oratory, a basilica worthy of receiving and watching over the treasure with which he had just enriched Christianity. This was the last honor that was missing in the world of St. Magdalene, and the greatest of all, since it was the most magnificent and the most popular. Eloquence and poetry are less subject to pass away than a monument, but both speak only to cultured minds, in books that are always rare, and that fall only in privileged hands. The monument addresses itself to the eyes and to the heart of everyone. The poor man has his place as well as the rich man; the common man can admire it as much as the artist. Thus, every lofty thought will always seek to express itself by an imposing monument. From the tower of Babel to the temple of Solomon, from the temple of Solomon to the basilica of St. Peter, people were seen creating in marble or granite, representations as memorable as possible of their love and of their faith. It was appropriate, then, that the friend of Jesus had some part of the earth worthy of her. It could not be better than the burial place where she had lain for thirteen centuries, there where piety had discovered her body, and near the mountain where she had completed her life in the highest mysteries of contemplation.

As early as 1295, Charles called for a plan and began work. It was to be in basilica form, that is to say, a building of three long naves without a cross, because such was the shape of the primitive oratory which it was to replace. But at the same time, all the details of the structure bore the character of a Gothic ship, to have it faithful to both periods, antiquity and modern times.

Despite his fervent generosity, Charles II did not complete the monument in which he had placed his heart; it was the work of all his family during two centuries. When the second to last of his successors as count of Provence and the kingdom of Naples, good King René, died in 1480 he had the pleasure of seeing the church and the monastery almost completed, as they are tody. It was also the end marked by Providence of the sovereign house of Anjou, as if it had been called to the throne to give St. Mary Magdalene all the brilliance that piety and generosity, transmitted from reign to reign for long generations, could convey to it. There was no prince of that family who did not visit, in his various fortunes, the

Sainte-Baume and St. Maximinus, confirmed the privileges, and gave a hand in completing the basilica. It was finally built after two hundred years of efforts, as posterity sees it today, a monument of severe and simple art, where grace unites with grandeur, and in which, in that lonely plain, at the foot of those steep mountains, between poor homes, few in number, there appears a stranded ship that awaits a powerful hand to launch it on the waves. The waves did come, in fact; they came from people agitated to their depths. Revolutions, after kings and popes, visited the basilica of St. Magdalene; those thunder claps that had beaten down thrones did not growl over the humble friend of the feet of the Savior except to respect its roof. Bethany is no more, but Jesus Christ has given to Magdalene the house she lost and both, the Master and the disciple, God and the woman He cherished, inhabit St. Maximinus together, as before along the sides of the Mount of Olives. Marseille is the Jerusalem of this new Bethany, and France is its Judea, greater and more faithful.

I say: France; it was indeed France that inherited Provence, and with it, St. Magdalene. One could have feared that the latter part of the inheritance would have been neglected and that our kings had not understood the gift that Providence had given them. No such thing. Louis XI, the first who united the crown of the Capetiens with that of the counts of Provence, gave the example of boundless veneration for St.

Magdalene. He treated her as a daughter of France, and bequeathed his pilgrimage to his descendants as the pilgrimage appropriate for the French monarchy. Charles VIII and Louis XII gloried in imitating him. Anne of Brittany, wife of one and then of the other, visited St. Maximinus and the *Sainte-Baume*, and had herself represented by a golden statuette at the feet of the reliquary that held the head of St. Magdalene. Francis Ist, after the battle of Marignan, went there in thanksgiving, with his mother, his wife, and his sister. He had the residence for travelers at *Sainte-Baume* repaired and wished that three apartments be built to accommodate the three highest persons of the court. These apartments were named *chamber of the king, chamber of the queen, and chamber of the dauphin.* That of the king was set in the very interior of the convent inhabited by the religious. That same prince embellished with a portico the entrance to the grotto. His successors Charles IX and Louis XIII followed him and discovered these traces of royal generosity. Louis XIII came in 1622, after the siege of Montpellier and the submission of the heretics of Languedoc.

The last king of France who made the pilgrimage to the holy places of Provence was Louis XIV. He arrived at St. Maximinus on 4 February 1660, with his mother, Anne of Austria, and on the following day climbed to the *Sainte-Baume* and the *Sacred Pillar*. On his return, he presided at the transfer of the body of St.

Magdalene into an urn of porphyry that had been
sent from Rome by the General of the Friars
Preachers. This was placed on the main altar, after
the reliquary that was to hold it was opened,
closed, and sealed in the presence of the king.
Thus, at the moment when the monarchy reached
the summit of its splendor and inscribed one of
the centuries of France among the greatest
centuries of the world, it arrived in the person of
the king who had the pleasure of giving his name
to that memorable era. He bowed down before the
remains of the humble penitent of Bethany and
left there a ray of that majesty that is still called,
and will always be called, the century of Louis
XIV.

What was left to do to accomplish the
promise of Jesus Christ? It had been sixteen
centuries that a ship had taken Mary Magdalene to
the soil of France. Since that time, a succession of
remarkable events, one after the other, confirmed
and increased the magnificence of devotion to her.
The *Sainte-Baume*, where Jesus Christ had
resumed with her the conversations interrupted at
the Holy Sepulcher, had become one of the
mountains made famous by the visit from God.
Magdalene had received nearby, from the hands of
an apostolic bishop, a burial that was never
forgotten. Moreover, the alabaster jar in which her
body was placed — more durable than the one
from which she had poured perfume on the feet of
the Savior — found in time and in men nothing
but the immortality of respect. It subsists again

today on the same earth and under the same sky. Holy caretakers were assigned to it as soon as the persecutions were ended and allowed piety to stand tall and visible at the door of the famous tombs. When Europe rose up to reconquer the first of these tombs, the closer one, where Mary Magdalene herself had watched, Christian chivalry adopted her as its special lady. Her name, carried in the heart of the crusaders, died on their lips with supernatural honor on the fields of battle. An entire family of princes was finally consecrated to her service. The first among them discovered her body, hidden for a long time our of fear of the barbarians, and brought it to a light more splendid than had ever been seen. The scars of the friendship with God on her forehead appeared to be living, and on seeing them, unspeakable tears streamed from the eyes of the most worthy to shed them. A basilica illustrious by its size and beauty was built over the well-beloved relics, made dearer by their absence; succeeding kings and popes were vying with each other. On a single day, there were five kings and a century brought eight popes.

(Author's note: In 1322, Philip de Valois, king of France; Alphonsus IX, king of Aragon; Hugh IV, king of Cyprus; John of Luxemburg, king of Bohemia; Robert, king of Sicily.

Popes: John XXII, Benedict XII, Clement VI, Innocent VI, Urban V, Gregory XI, Clement VII, Benedict XIII.)

When it was completed, the blood of St. Louis, who had given to Magdalene's tomb the counts of Provence and the kings of Sicily, finally gave it the kings of France. The premier monarchy of the world became protector and patron of the friend of Jesus Christ. At long last, having reached the summit of human greatness, and when it was on the eve of experiencing a catastrophe as startling was its past prosperity, there came a king even greater than the others, to represent all of them. This one, son of the glory and piety of his ancestors, brought to the tomb that they had honored the final homage of France.

Was it indeed the last? That was believable. A mocking skepticism had overcome minds, and an unheard of revolution was to overturn under its feet, along with the throne of France, even the throne of God. But, while the most venerable sanctuaries did not escape the storm, a special protection covered the monastery and the basilica of St. Maximinus. A previously unknown man, whose name would soon grow beyond all measure, — the brother of a young captain destined one day to reopen the temples and fill the world with the surprises of his glory — Lucien Bonaparte, was the savior of these two monuments erected by the faith of princes and of people to the love of Mary Magdalene. Not one stone fell from their respected bulk, not one altar was destroyed, not one painting disappeared from their walls. When divine anger, appeased by so many misfortunes, left us, an astonished France found still standing the work of nephews and sons of St. Louis, having as its title the name of a new family and the beginning of another history. The relics of St. Magdalene themselves had not perished; the head and the bone of the right arm, piously retrieved by a faithful hand, were authentically recognized; but if the gold and the precious stones were missing from this treasure, the grace of God, manifested by so many marvels, lived on more animated than ever. Less fortunate, the *Sainte-Baume* experienced the outrages of ruthless devastation; all that was left was the bluff itself and a part of its forest. At first repaired, ravaged anew in 1815, it was finally blessed solemnly in May 1822, the Monday after Pentecost, in the presence of more than forty thousand men, flocking to this scene that bore witness so boldly to the impotence of ruins against God. From the height of the terrace facing the *Sainte-Baume*, the archbishop of Aix raised his hand with the sacred host over the multitude that covered the plain and the forest; the sign of the cross fell in an absolute silence over the place and the men who together and once again found Jesus Christ, conqueror of the world. An immense cheer, from forty thousand mouths, suddenly followed the religious silence of the blessing. The centuries, reanimated by this cry of faith, could hear in eternity, where all of them return, the deep echo of this festival given by so many souls to the soul of Mary Magdalene.

(Author's note: reconstruction of the *SainteBaume* was

96

due principally to M. de Villeneuve-Bargemont, chief administrator of Bouches-duRhône, and M. Chevalier, chief administrator of the Var.)

When a stranger comes down the river that divides Paris, he encounters a place whose size and monuments invite his meditation. On one side, it is the palace of the kings of France, and facing it, at the end of a long avenue, a military triumphal arch. In a second view, that bisects the first in the form of a cross two temples harmonize with each other: one is the temple of law, the other the temple of God. In the center stands an Egyptian obelisk, but that disappears before a monument invisibly present to all minds: the scaffold of Louis XVI. All France lies in that area: royalty, the glory of arms, liberty, religion, revolution. Now if one approaches the temple that is like the part of God in this representation of the country, one can read there: *To the very good and very great God, under the invocation of St. Mary Magdalene.* Mary Magdalene is there, under the eyes of France and of the world, in the 19th century of Christ; the triumphal place it occupies, a conqueror, a man uplifted by fate to the summit of human matters, had destined it to receive, in marble, bronze, gold, the names of his battles and the images of his soldiers. He himself was to preside in a kind of apotheosis, to this pantheon of his person, that he had anticipated calling, by the audacity of pride: *the Temple of Glory.* In its place, after he suddenly fell, there came the humble penitent who washed with her tears the feet of Jesus Christ. We can see her on the façade, kneeling as long ago before her Master; inside, under a splendid vault, she seems to be carried by angels in the elation of ecstasy that was, even here below, the price of her love.

With the infinite tenderness of Providence, this temple contains not only the glory of Magdalene, but also part of her mortal remains, oddly escaped from an expected loss. In 1785, the Infanta of Spain, Ferdinand, Duke of Parma, wanted a portion of the holy relics for his chapel. Louis XVI, to whom he had expressed his wish, ordered the religious of St. Maximinus to satisfy him. Accordingly, the urn of porphyry wherein Louis XIV had transferred the ancient reliquary, was opened with all appropriate precautions and solemnities. The prior removed a bone of considerable size and carried it himself to the Duke of Parma. Now in 1810, this treasure along with many others, was brought to Paris following our conquests and, after having passed from the hands of one exiled cardinal to those of Venerable Mme Soyecourt, superior of the Carmelites on Vaugirard Street, it was finally ceded to Mgr de Quélen, archbishop of Paris, who gave it as a gift to the church of St. Magdalene.

And so, of the three portions that Charles II of Anjou had made of the major relics, namely, the head, a bone of the right arm, and the rest of the bones, the first two were saved from the revolution and never left St. Maximinus. The third, placed by Louis XIV in the urn of porphyry of the main altar, disappeared; but as we have said, a part of it, and to Louis XIV's urn of porphyry that had contained it, there followed the most magnificent temple ever erected on earth in honor of the penitent of Bethany.

Thus, this glory has not only crossed the centuries, it grew with them, despite all events. I do not know if in the history of saints there is any other example of such persevering and divine change. And yet the guard that had been placed on the tomb of the saint and had never missed its watch for a single day in fifteen hundred years, that guard no longer existed. The basilica was still standing with its monastery, with its crypt and its tombs, with its relics preserved, with great memories of a life that goes back to the cradle of Christianity, and is tied to the memory of Jesus Christ. It remains standing; yet the pilgrim does not enter it without a yearning and without a sigh. Astonished, he looks at this mass, immobile, victorious over men more than over the ages, and it seems to him that it penetrates the silence of the desert rather than the silence of God. On both knees, he prayed to this important and saintly friend of the redemption of souls whom he came to visit; on leaving, he saw everywhere her picture, her name, her glory, her virtue. For all that, the anointing of his prayer was not without sadness, similar to the tears one sheds at a cherished place, but where something is missing that the heart had seen there and would like to find again. Oh, the goodness of God over our desires!

With our eyes, we have seen the empty cloister repopulated, the ancient ceremonies take up their interrupted harmony, the past come out of its tomb with a youthfulness we did not think it capable of — and we believed we heard Jesus Christ tell his loyal friend who could not believe in his resurrection, the word of reproach and of enlightenment: *Mary!*

EPILOGUE

The tomb of Mary Magdalene at St. Maximinus is the third tomb of the world. It comes immediately after the tomb of Our Savior in Jerusalem and that of St. Peter in Rome. This is because the most holy Virgin, Mother of God, had no sepulcher among men, and was barely touched by death. She was enraptured by His power in the triumph of her assumption. Neither did St. John, the beloved disciple, leave for the veneration of Christians his bones or his tomb. He was, by leave from God, deprived of this glory so as to survive as if buried in his Gospel. Thus, there remain on earth only three important tombs: that of the Savior, removed by barbarians from the liberty of our homage, but which has kept in its charge sovereignty over the world; that of the apostle St. Peter which presides in Rome over the destinies of Christianity and which, from the dust that hides its incredible splendors, sees and hears pass by the continuous prayers of generations; finally, that of Mary Magdalene, less high than St. Peter in the hierarchy, but closer to Jesus Christ by her heart, and to whom no one can dispute this third place in the important names of the evangelical age.

Here perhaps, at the end of our work, the question could be asked why the divine Master of souls wanted to choose to love Him by preference a lowly sinner, and to bequeath her to us as a model of holiness. The reason is not difficult to understand: innocence is a drop of water in the world, repentance is the ocean that envelops it and that saves. It was therefore worthy of the goodness of God to raise repentance as high as possible; that is why, in the Old Testament as in the New, He placed under our eyes a victorious model of rehabilitation brought about by penance, David and Mary Magdalene. We could have believed that David could not be surpassed, so much had his figure been traced with tenderness and depth. A simple shepherd watching over his sheep on the hills of Bethlehem, he became a soldier in the presence of an injury to God by his country, to Jehovah. His sling struck down the blasphemer; moreover, sparkling in his victory, he gained in one day the heart of the people. But jealousy, the companion of heroes, did not delay in appearing between the glory and himself. Even the king envied his youth, and tormented by the foreboding of his fame, he pondered his loss in an attack of threatening depression. It was then that David, to calm him down, picked up, for the first time, the harp that was to sing all the mysteries of God and echo in the hearts of generations. Poetry united itself with courage in his fate. With friendship, misfortune and religion also adding themselves, the young man finally mounted the throne that ever after was to be called the throne of David. There, at the height of his prosperity, blessed by God more than were Abraham, Isaac, and Jacob, and predestined ancestor of Christ, he suddenly fell into adultery, treason, and homicide. A fortunate fall since it made of the guilty man, the immortal king of repentance, and gave all of us, sinners who come after him, tears for our faults and a measure to carry our tears all the way to God. Who, among Christians, has not wept with David? Who has not found in his poetry, the soothing balm that his heart needed? The Gospel itself could not erase the psalms; this king, dishonored for his crime, is at every moment the father of our virtues.

This was, in the Old Testament, the model of repentance. Surely, no one could have foreseen that God, in the New Testament, would place alongside Jesus Christ, another and more divine figure of repentance. And yet He succeeded! Mary Magdalene was an unpretentious woman without any history except for her sin; she had neither spear, nor sword, nor harp, nor the eye of prophets. She was a sinner like so many others. Only once in the Gospel does she speak, at the tomb of her Master, and her words have no luster. But, first of all, she was a woman, that is to say, the being in whom the stain is most irreversible. This difference between the Old and the New Testaments is for her alone a sublime development in mercy. It is no longer a male who has redeemed himself by repentance, it is a female. Before Jesus Christ, no woman struck down by vice was lifted up. Jesus Christ was the only one to bring this about.

Holding to his work, He followed the sinful woman patiently throughout the ages, to save her glory, to revive and rejuvenate it always. David sang his repentance with unequaled poetry; this poetry created his immortality. Mary Magdalene had only her tears, but they flowed on the feet of the Savior; she had but a jar of perfume, but this perfume anointed the body of the Son of God. The simplicity here is much greater, the tenderness deeper; it is no longer a male who weeps and who loves, it is a female, a woman who has seen God, who recognized Him, and in comparing His infinite purity to the degradation to which she had fallen, did not doubt that she could be pardoned by the power of love. Humble and hidden after having found grace, she did not stray far from the feet that purified her. She used the familiarity she gained to follow and serve only Jesus Christ. She followed Him up to the cross, up to tomb. Separated from her Master, the unique objective of her life, she withdrew from the places where she had lived with Him and, seeking a haven against the last traces of the world, she buried her memories and her soul in another. Only angels were able to discover it, and brought her from on high the invisible manna that causes ecstasy and rapture. Finally, she died of love, having received from a bishop sent by God the sacred body of the Son of God.

And now, what I can say? Those places so famous and so venerated that I have described, that grotto, that tomb, that crypt, that basilica, that monastery: this entire ensemble of monuments that nature and grace, that time and the princes had erected to the glory of Mary Magdalene, all of that is still standing, but impoverished, bare, desolate, covered with the wounds of a century that was satisfied with ruins, and like the others had been pleased in their erection. To reach the *Sainte-Baume*, one climbs the steps of a disfigured stairway, between crumbling walls; the apartment of the kings of France has disappeared, and the most humble pilgrim will have trouble finding shelter wherein to rest from the road. The hostel has retained only the openings in the rock wherein the joists of the framework rested. The convent, hastily restored, offers the religious rooms separated only by planks, which they share with strangers. Between these two, the grotto of repentance remains open, itself emptied of the ornaments that it owed to the centuries-old piety of people and princes. The splendid lamps that provided its light, no longer shine except by the striking absence about which Tacitus speaks. Marbles without glory form the chapel of the saint; behind its altar, on that mysterious rock where she passed her nights in ecstasy, rests half inclined a worldly statue, unworthy of the first head of the majesty of the place, all of whose memories it saddens.

If from the heights and the wretchedness of the *Sainte-Baume* we go back down to St. Maximinus, by the same route that the saint followed, so that we might look for her tomb, we will find the same contrast between destitution and magnificence. The basilica is impressively seated on its old site; it still commands the admiration of the artist and the homage of the Christian. But unfinished, right from its portico, it leads us with yearning towards the crypt where St. Maximinus had placed in alabaster the body of St. Magdalene. The alabaster is still there; beside it are still aligned the tombs that a fervent piety had eagerly desired and built near this significant tomb; but what desolation, what darkness, what sadness of heart and of the walls! Blessed are those catacombs that never experienced glory and who sleep silently in a mystery that was never disturbed! Here, every place is filled with knees that bend on the flagstones; everything expresses the antiquity of a veneration that was never interrupted. And yet, it is only thought that incurs the expenses of this magnificence; God does not appear save in the light of the soul. A coarse reliquary of wood, given by some peasants, covers the head where the brother of St. Louis, Charles I of Anjou, had placed the royal crown of Sicily, and at the feet of which Anne of Brittany, twice queen of France, had herself represented on her knees and in gold. An episcopal hand, it is true (Bishop Jordany of Fréjus and of Toulon), will cover these traces of an unfortunate time, and return to the forehead of Mary Magdalene some of the splendor that been attached there by men and by centuries. But how many painful traces are left to be repaired after that one! What troubles to cover! How many shadows to change!

Oh, whoever you are who read these pages — if ever you have known tears of repentance or tears of love — do not refuse Mary Magdalene, who wept so much and who loved so much, a drop of that perfume with which she anointed the feet of your Savior. Do not abandon the grotto where the angels visited her; do not forget the tomb where Jesus Christ concealed her against barbarian injuries to present her to the homage of Christian ages. Do not disregard this head that survived all the rest, because God Himself touched her with his finger. Bring your tribute, however meager, for the renovation of one of the most beloved monuments of Christianity. Bring to it your faith, your wishes, your needs. Let it not be said that France, to which Jesus Christ wished to entrust Mary Magdalene with the safekeeping of repentance and of love, was unfaithful to its holy mission. As for me, unworthy of it though I was, who brought to the mountain and to the basilica the ancient militia charged by Providence to watch day and night, may I write here my final lines, and like Mary Magdalene, on the day before the eve of the Passion, break at the feet of Jesus Christ the fragile but reliable jar of my thoughts!

Made in the USA
Columbia, SC
24 November 2024

47461758R00067